MONASTIC TREASURES
FOR ALL OF US

MONASTIC TREASURES FOR ALL OF US

A Series of Homiles and Lectures by the
Thrice-Blessed Pope Shenouda III
of Blessed Memory

ST MARY & MOSES ABBEY PRESS

CONTENTS

✠

In the Name of the Father, the Son, and the Holy Spirit,
One God. Amen.

We thank the Lord who has so kindly helped us along this
endeavor to provide the world with these first-fruits of an
English translation to a priceless treasure: *Monastic Treasures
for All of Us: A Series of Homilies and Lectures by the Thrice-
Blessed Pope Shenouda III of Blessed Memory*. Most, if not all, of
these homilies were delivered to monastic communities. His
Holiness truly needs no introduction, nor is his status as a
spiritual elder akin to the famed desert fathers of the fourth
century (the era of St. Anthony the Great) questionable. In
these homilies, His Holiness is speaking from over eighty
years of life experience and over fifty years of monastic
experience. He was first appointed a monk at St. Mary's
Monastery (El-Souryan), and thereafter ordained as a priest,
a hegumen, a bishop, and finally the 117th Pope and Patriarch
of Alexandria. He has been counseling and caring, mentoring
and monitoring, teaching and training, and guiding and giving
for all these years, acquiring experience all along the way.
Before us is a true guiding light on monasticism, to whom
discipleship is indispensable, in order to gradually master the
monastic life, or simply to be nurtured spiritually in everyday
life.

In an attempt to use gender inclusive language that is warm
and welcoming to all readers, we considered replacing "he or
she" with "person, one, or you" in most cases. We also tried,
as much as possible, to render a true yet dynamic translation,
in order to arrive at a smooth balance between an exact word-
for-word literal translation (which is oftentimes awkward or
unintelligible to readers) and a strictly paraphrased translation
(which sometimes loses the intended depth of the message).

We would like to thank all those who have labored in order
for these sermons to see the light, especially the translation
reviewers. We pray that we have reached our intention of
providing readers with an eloquent, fluent, and genuine
translation of the sermons, which the Lord uses for the glory
of His Holy Name. Glory be to God forever. Amen.

FATHER ANASTASI

In the Name of the Father, the Son, and the Holy Spirit,
One God. Amen.

To Fr. Anastasi's great shock, he awoke feeling a veil-like object on his face. As he lifted his hand to remove it, something fell out of his hand. As he felt for it, he realized that it was a cross. The place was shrouded in darkness, which puzzled Fr. Anastasi greatly since he remembered that the window to his cell was open when he lay down to sleep, and that the moonlight had filled the place, beaming light into the room. Also, what was this strange scent that he smelled? He tried to discover its source but was unable; it resembled the stench of death. With time his eyes began to adapt, so he tried to peer in the darkness, perhaps he could see. His hair stood on end in fear and shock, and his whole body trembled. He placed his palms over his eyes to block out the image, but when he removed them he found the same scene: piles of bones lay in the corners, and corpses laid out on the floor around him. Each one was dressed in a white tunic with a veil on his face and a cross in his hand. No doubt he was in the monastery catacombs!

An eerie notion seized him, which he unsuccessfully tried to dismiss. In a spontaneous motion, he looked at himself and found that he also was dressed in a white tunic, and as far as he could see his beard was all white. There had only been three or four white hairs before. He realized the shocking reality: he was in the monastery catacombs. But what happened to him? Did he really die and God raised him from the dead? Did the monks wrongly assume him to be dead and bury him? Is there a third explanation? He did not know. The compelling reality before him was that, at least as far as people were concerned, he was dead. He also realized another truth: he could not come out of this condition. How could people see before them a dead person whom they buried with their own hands? Their nerves would not handle it, neither would their minds. Therefore, he must spend the rest of his life as a dead person inside the tomb. This was a new trial for him in life. How will he live this way?

On the first day, he was greatly afflicted. The terrible putrefying stench was unbearable, but he told himself, "I am supposed to have left the luxuries of the world, and I must live this way." He remembered the story of St. Arsenius, who did not replace the water used for soaking his palms until it stank, claiming that its stench was in exchange for the sweet scents with which he had indulged in the imperial palace. Soon, Fr. Anastasi grew accustomed to this condition of living among the bones and bearing with that stench.

There remained before him the issue of food. How will he eat? There was no food with him in the tomb, and he was unable to bring food from the monastery and preserve it. Rather, he left each night in the dark, about midnight, and ate some fruits or vegetables from the monastery's garden, or some leftover food in a plate that the cook had forgotten to wash. Perhaps a loaf and a little salt, this sufficed. He remained fasting all day until midnight came. Thus, he spent many years with the sun never seeing him eating. In fact, the sun did not see him at all.

In the tomb, he had no kitchenware or plates. Here Fr. Anastasi remembered how he had kept tens of kitchen utensils and various plates and dishes in his cell. Now he had none of these and was surviving without them, just as St. Pijimi the anchorite who lived with absolutely no utensils in his cave. Here Fr. Anastasi felt ashamed over his former life.

His conscience began to rebuke him. How did he, being a monk, own many such utensils which had seemed necessary to him at that time and which he had now practically proven that he could live without? He remembered the tens of other tools that he kept in his cell at that time: desk supplies, furnishings, pictures, clothing, covers, and many miscellaneous items. His conscience chastened him greatly over this. What was the meaning of poverty to which he had vowed on the day of his ordination? Where was the virtue of detachment? He explored within himself the issue of necessities and luxuries. Undoubtedly, it was relative, depending on an individual's level of detachment and valuation of necessities.

As for now, Fr. Anastasi was able to live in the monastery, owning absolutely nothing at all, living a life of complete detachment.

Even the cell (his personal dwelling), now he lived in the tomb which he could not consider as his own personal cell. He was a stranger, even in this place. Formerly, he had a cell with an inner room that no one could enter without his permission. He could lock or unlock his cell as he pleased with a key which he kept with him. As for now, he had no control over his dwelling place. If they interred a new person, he could not object or open his mouth. Rather, as soon as he heard the sad chimes of the monastery bells, he rushed to assume his former position as a corpse and covered his face with his veil, so that when the monks opened the catacomb to place the new corpse, they would find everything as they had left it.

Fr. Anastasi could not even own books. How then did he spend his time? Here he began to realize his former mistake. At that time, his goal was to fill his mind with information. He would read tens of books and became an encyclopedia, but perhaps he had no time to meditate on what he had read. Now, having no books, he began to ruminate on the information stored in his memory, and meditate. Sometimes, he would dwell on one verse for some days, diving into its depth, the Spirit revealing to him amazing mysteries, to the point that he would cry out in joy with David the Prophet, "I have seen the consummation of all perfection, but Your commandments are exceedingly broad." He realized that he had formerly lived on the shallow and superficial level of knowledge. Now when he had a craving to read, he would go in the darkness to the church, read shortly in calmness, and then returns to the catacombs.

Fr. Anastasi lived a life of complete isolation and silence. Naturally, he visited no one and no one visited him. He lived in complete silence, conversing with no one. Once, some monks were talking outside the catacombs. He heard their voices but did not comment as to whether the information they said was true or false, complete or partial. It was not for him to intervene. How would this concern him, he was dead! Another time, he heard monks outside the catacombs speaking of the forefathers and his name came up; some had good memories of him, while others criticized him. As for him, he remained silent, not thanking the one who praised him, nor arguing with the one who criticized him; he was dead.

Once, Fr. Anastasi fell sick, and naturally, no doctor visited him. He took no medicine or any type of treatment, nutrition, or supplements. He endured in stillness and silence. Not even a kind word reached him, since no one visited him. And if he sensed anyone outside the tomb, he did not even permit a groan. He remained this way until he recovered.

Once, as he walked at night, two monks saw him. One shrieked and fled, while the other—assuming him an anchorite or one of the old saints—approached him and knelt down, asking his blessing. He did not argue, but obeyed, and placed his hand on him and blessed him, then quickly raced toward the tomb. Thus, it was rumored in the monastery that a saint had appeared to some of the monks. Fr. Anastasi secluded himself for several days thereafter (not leaving his tomb at all); he remained without food or drink.

Fr. Anastasi lived completely remote to the world. In his former life, he would write letters to many and receive replies. Now that he was dead, he was cut off from the letters, the magazines, the newspapers, and news altogether. No world news, church news, or even monastery news reached him. With time, he even began to forget the old news as well. Formerly, he felt that the monastery needed him, and that he was one of the pillars of the monastery, an important person who held many responsibilities. Now, he learned that the monastery continues without him. Likewise, sometimes positions and responsibilities were vacant in the church, but no one nominated him for them; he was dead. He likewise did not think of these issues, nor was he aware of them.

Since he had nothing to preoccupy him except God, he lived a life of unceasing prayer. Before his death, he had spent many nights reading, writing, translating, transcribing, and was busy with many other issues, but now, he was unable to read or write at night since there are no books or lighting.

Therefore, he spent the entire night in prayer, remembering St. Isaac's saying, "The night is set apart to engage in prayer." He also used the night to perform his necessary functions in the monastery.

He progressed in prayer greatly, until his entire life turned into prayer. Nothing remained in his mind except God. With time, he forgot the old memories. As no new worldly things were added to it, his subconscious was being purified of all that remained in it of world news, its memories, and its preoccupations. Thus, distraction vanished from his prayers and he began to reach purity of heart and purity of thought; released from all and joined to the One.

He was purified of sinful thoughts, but one thought continued to war against him. He told himself, "Behold, now I have learned true monasticism, and engaged in complete death to the world and full unity with God, so what prevents me from appearing to the monastery and living thus?"

What urged him on this thought was the long time he had spent in the tomb, so that people had forgotten him. Many of his old friends were buried alongside him in the tomb. Most of the monks now in the monastery were new who had not known him. His friends who remained alive were few, and they would not expect to see him. Also, if they did see him, they would not recognize him, because his appearance had changed due to his aging and asceticism.

Fr. Anastasi tried to expel this thought. He told himself, "What benefit is it for people to see me? In my former life, I longed to live alone and away from people, set apart for God alone, and now I have what I wanted, so why would I think of changing my condition?" Then the thoughts would return to war against him saying, "You did this by compulsion, but how wonderful for you to do it willfully." A long time passed in battling these thoughts.

Finally, a very critical night in his life came. On that night, the thoughts became overbearing, so Fr. Anastasi knelt down and poured himself out before God in intense fervor, saying, "Blessed are You God in all Your goodness to me. Lord, You are very tender and compassionate towards me. You have treated me better than I deserve to be treated, and have given me this isolated life. You have released me from all and have allowed me to bond with You. I only feel that I have lived this life against my will. I want to live it willfully, out of my love for You. Is it a thought, or is it a desire? Is it good, or is it bad? In all cases, I present it before You because I am unable to hide anything from You. May Your will be done." Fr. Anastasi lowered his head and wept. No one heard him, but heaven heard. One of the twenty-four priests seated around the throne of God came forward and took this prayer in his golden censer and ascended above with it. Fr. Anastasi fell asleep, with his tears wetting his white beard.

He did not know how much time passed as he slept. Was it an hour or an age? All he knew was that he heard a bell ring sharply; it was the bell for midnight praises he heard every night in the tomb. Fr. Anastasi opened his eyes in great shock, asking, "What is this that I see?" He turned his head and fell asleep. He awoke on the sound of another bell, perhaps the bell for the Prime hour. He opened his eyes, and behold, to his shocking amazement, he was before the first scene. He found before him an open window with the moonlight exuding the entire place. He looked to himself and found that he was dressed in black. He looked around, and found that it resembled that cell he had lived in, in that time, so he placed his hand on his head and began to think. Finally, he understood the mystery... Was what had happened to him a dream, a vision, or a lesson in monasticism? He did not know, but he understood the lesson intended.

From that moment on, his life changed completely. He began the life of isolation and asceticism which he had learned during those tens of years. He took on unceasing prayer as he had practiced it in the tomb. When he was compelled to leave his cell for a service to the community, he walked calmly, not looking to the left or to the right. The monks recognized him by his silence and his emaciated body, his gentle demeanor and humility, and by his head being always bowed down. From time to time, he would slightly lift his head, shaking it slightly to shake off drops of tears preventing him from looking ahead.

Glory be to God forever. Amen.

EARTHLY ANGELS: SPIRITUAL BEINGS

In the Name of the Father, the Son, and the Holy Spirit,
One God. Amen.

Introduction

This evening I would like to meditate with you on one nickname given to monastics. Monastics are nicknamed "earthly angels," because each monastic is considered an angel. Here I would like to discuss the meaning of the term angel, and why monastics are identified as such. The first characteristic is that angels are spiritual beings, or more precisely actual spirits: "Who makes His angels spirits, His ministers a flame of fire."[1] The monastic who is an angel, lives as a spirit, by the spirit, remote from the body and bodily deeds, and remote from materialism. To what extent is the monastic a spirit, behaving as a spirit, by the spirit, or according to the spirit? How could a monastic refuse all bodily deeds? This is by avoiding all carnal desires.

Food

Among the common carnal desires is the craving for food, therefore, monastics are fasting ascetics who disregard the demands of their bodies. When St. Macarius the Alexandrian visited the monasteries of St. Pachomius and practiced such unusual fasting during the Great Fast, the monks were disturbed. They told St. Pachomius, "He's not even flesh and blood!"[2] It is not the manner of a bodily person to fast in this fashion; he fasted all week, eating only once a week. Angels do not eat; they have no bodily discharge.

---

1   Ps 104:4
2   (Behr 2004), 147.

The more a person subdues the body in food, the greater the opportunities given to the spirit. Even secular persons, such as Yogis, subdue the body greatly in fasting, so that the spirit has greater opportunity for purification, because the body eclipses the spirit, and overeating weighs down the spirit, not allowing it breathing room. I remember how Fr. Abdelmesih the Ethiopian would move about the desert as a gazelle. He was a featherweight, and even his movements were light.

Craving Food

Monastics are angels in the sense of their lack of concern for bodily demands of food. I wish you would read how the fathers behaved towards food and fasting. When St. Arsenius began picking the good beans he took a good lesson from Abba Isaiah, therefore he said, "I have indeed been taught Latin and Greek, but I do not know even the alphabet of this peasant."[3] Observe the fathers' attitude towards abstinence from food, specific foods, and desirable foods, of which they say, "Withdraw your hand while your soul still crave it."[4] They did not allow themselves to enjoy food, as one of the Fathers said, "If you are offered food that you crave, spoil it slightly, and then eat," change its taste, blend it with something, add salt. From here, complaining over food or requesting specific types of food were not monastic spiritual characteristics.

Chastity

Chastity and physical purity are among the features where monastics are alien to the body; this is one of the three vows of monasticism: obedience, chastity, and voluntary poverty. For monastics, chastity is at a higher level than for seculars, because monastics are completely chaste beings. Even in clothing, their entire body is covered, no part is revealed in any way. A monastic should avoid improper over-familiarity.

---

3   (Ward, Sayings 1984), 10.
4   (Chryssavgis and Penkett, Abba Isaiah 2002), 57.

St. Isaac said, "One maintains bodily chastity and modesty even inside the cell,"[5] in apparel, in the way one sits, in the way one sleeps, and so forth. If engaged in a mental warfare, a monastic should not follow through with the suggested thought, but should resist it, even if to death. St. Paul the apostle's expression is very beautiful; in rebuking the Hebrews he said, "You have not yet resisted to bloodshed, striving against sin."[6] That means, if it is called for, one would prefer martyrdom rather than sinning in the flesh. The monastic is an angel, as if absolutely without a physical body. Regarding chastity, the farthest extent a monastic might reach is mental, but to reach the physical level is alien to monastics. A monastic should resist impure thoughts with all possible might, and also avoid the sources of those thoughts.

Vigil

The monastic is an angel in regards to the body: food, chastity, and vigil. One does not give the body its demands of food, bodily desire, or rest in sleep. Before us stands the saying of our Lord: "The spirit indeed is willing, but the flesh is weak."[7] We find that the church helps the monastic keep vigil by the three watches of the Midnight Prayer and the Psalmody (Tasbeha). Most likely, the monastic who does not attend Psalmody is asleep, which means yielding to the body. This is not a monastic behavior, unless this monastic has a special arrangement with the confession father, keeps vigil until a very late hour and offers the spiritual duties in a special way, akin to the solitaries. Monastics who keep vigil in prayer resemble the angels, but those who sleep forfeit the work of the angel and fall under bodily control—the body takes over through food, wars against chastity, rest, and sleep.

---

5   Cf. (Miller 1984), 54–55.
6   Heb 12:4
7   Mt 26:41; Mk 14:38

Resisting Rest

As angels, monastics not only resisted sleep, but even rest. They struggled to fatigue the body, the ancients advised us to tax the body to the limit of endurance. How did monastics crucify the flesh with its passions?[8] How did they fatigue their bodies? This is amply available in the Hagiography (lives of the saints). Among the most distinctive examples in the history of monasticism are the Stylite Fathers. St. Simon the Stylite, St. Luke the Stylite, and the rest of the Stylites fatigued their bodies in an unparalleled way. It is the same when a person stands for prayer without allowing the body any rest, or one who fatigues the body in serving the brethren or the monastery. The body should be a slave to the person's will and spirit; it should not be allowed to make specific demands. Otherwise, what then would be the meaning of angels? Angels are spirits. If we come to say that these are earthly angels, meanwhile, they are living according to the flesh and the comforts of the flesh; then the angel is not clear here at all.

Appearance

Each one of you should ask yourself: "Do I please my body in a specific way? Do I please it in sleep, in rest, in food, in bodily desire, in embellishment and appearance?" Sometimes the new monastic image engages the monastic in a struggle: wanting to have a stylish appearance. This is also one of the bodily wars: embellishment or stylishness. Monastics should be completely remote from this issue.

---

8   Heb 5:24

Toil

Among those who fatigued their bodies greatly was St. Paul of Tammoh, to whom the Lord Christ appeared (due to his excessive bodily exhaustion) saying: "Enough exhaustion my beloved Paul." To which St. Paul replied, "My Lord, no matter how hard I exhaust myself, it does not compare with Your toil for us." (St. Paul of Tammoh is the one buried beside St. Bishoy.)[9] Let us compile, from within *The Paradise of the Holy Fathers* and Hagiography, a monastic's relationship with the body: victory over the flesh; denying bodily demands by means of vigil, physical toil, chastity, or fasting; and remoteness from embellishment. "One of the fathers asked Abba John the Dwarf, 'What is a monk?' He said, 'He is toil.'"[10] Monks who gave milder advice recommended toil by measure—the measure that a person is able to bear.[11]

Mortification

Prostrations were among the means by which they exhausted their bodies. Fasting, accompanied by many prostrations, was among the many means of crucifying the flesh. Our Catholic brethren call them Mortifications. St. Paul the apostle wrote regarding the flesh saying, "For your sake we are killed all day long,"[12] and, "Death is working in us."[13] Also, in the ninth hour litany we say, "Mortify our carnal senses, O Christ our God and deliver us." You all pray this, but has anyone thought what this means: "Mortify our carnal senses?" I want to leave this for your reflection. It means the senses should not have spirit-vexing activities: image-collecting eye, listening ear, and so forth.

---

9   (St. Mark and St. Bishoy Coptic Orthodox Church 1987), 69; René Basset, Patrologia Orientalis 1.3, no. 3, 322.
10   (Ward, Sayings 1984), 93.
11   Abba Poemen, Abba Pistamon Cf. (Ward, Sayings 1984), 177, 200.
12   Rom 8:36
13   2 Cor 4:12

Guarding the Senses

The person who falls obedient to the senses becomes a bodily person, and not a spiritual one. Therefore, among the most renowned monastic virtues is guarding the senses from straying in every direction. Many times what monastics' ears hear disturb them and destroy their spiritualities; their tongues might disturb them and likewise disturb others. Their eyes could also disturb them from the images they gather. Therefore, one advice given about guarding the senses is "Should you go into your superior's cell, or your friend's or disciple's, restrain your eyes so as not to see anything therein."[14] You should enter the cell and leave as if you had not seen anything, because you might see the cell and comment on that person's needs, possessions, or way of living; this is a never-ending issue. The first characteristic of the earthly angels is the issue of the body and the monastic's relationship with the body.

Purity of Heart

The second characteristic of angels is purity of heart, therefore, in referring to the monastic St. John Climacus says, "The monk is the pure heart."[15] Purity of heart is also accompanied by the purity of thoughts and assumptions. A suspicious person, a doubtful person, or a person whose thoughts are unsettled could not be pure. Monasticism is purity of the heart; if we elaborate on the purity of heart, it would encompass the entire life of holiness. The person whose heart is pure also has pure speech: "For out of the abundance of the heart the mouth speaks."[16] The pure-hearted person also has pure senses—not sinning through the senses. In every deed you do, in order to judge if it is good or evil, ask yourself, "If there were an angel in my place, would he do what I do? Would my guarding angel, or the angel who encompasses me, be ashamed of my deeds?" The psalm says,

---

14   St. Isaac the Syrian (Miller 1984), 94.
15   Cf. (Payne 1982), 233.
16   Mt 12:34

"Nor stands in the path of sinners, nor sits in the seat of the scornful"[17]—in applying this verse, would the angel be disturbed to find himself standing next to me?

Obedience

Among the other characteristics specific to angels, besides purity of heart, is obedience. Therefore we say in the Lord's Prayer, "Your will be done on earth as it is in heaven"; as Your will is fulfilled by the angels, may it be fulfilled by us. How do angels obey? Angels obey the command exactly as it is given, without arguing, quickly, and without delay. Psalm 103 says, "Bless the Lord, you His angels, who excel in strength, who do His word, heeding the voice of His word."[18] Angels obey exactly as our Lord commands, without arguing; if our Lord commands an angel to kill all the firstborn, he obeys without arguing, he does not question: "Is it right to kill all the firstborn? Is this out of compassion? Does it agree with mercy?" There is no arguing, his job is to follow orders, not to plan or argue. If at any command coming to you, you think and argue whether it is correct or not, then you have not become an angel; you might have become a planner, a leader, or a manager, but you have not become an angel. An angel obeys without arguing, and quickly. Perhaps a monastic hears a command and consents, but performs it the next day; this one is not obedient. Obedience means immediate execution of orders.

Conclusion

We said monastics are angels, as spiritual beings, who avoid the flesh and materialism (we have not spoken about materialism; this would need a special session; under this category fall love of possessions and love of worldly materials). We spoke about angels in the sense of purity of heart, and obedience.

---

17   Ps 1:1
18   Ps 103:20

Let us conclude with this topic for now. I remember a simple expression regarding the monastic's relationship with matter—how angels rise above the level of materialism—one saint said, "There is a monk who sells the whole world, and all its possessions, and comes to fight with his friend over a needle."[19] Has this person died to the world? Is this an angel? Ask yourself, "In my actions, do I act like an angel? If an angel were in my place, would he do what I do?"

Glory be to God forever. Amen.

---

19   Cf. (Payne 1982), 190.

EARTHLY ANGELS: UNCEASING PRAYER

In the Name of the Father, the Son, and the Holy Spirit,
One God. Amen.

Monastics were nicknamed earthly angels for two main reasons: the first is for purity of heart, and the second is for unceasing prayer. If you show mercy, seculars could be merciful; if you educate, seculars could educate; if you labor in service, seculars could labor in service; any virtue you mention, seculars could undertake. The one task seculars are unable to do is to pray unceasingly. Those who turned to monasticism did so for this very reason—the life of unceasing prayer. For the sake of unceasing prayer monks lived in solitude; the solitary life was not the intended purpose in and of itself, but was a means to unceasing prayer.

Therefore, when St. Arsenius was asked why he fled even from the saints (St. Macarius the Alexandrian asked him, "Why do you flee from us Father?"), St. Arsenius responded that he could not speak with God and with people at the same time.[20] A person who seeks to be isolated to speak with God, will arrive at solitude, and from there onto silence. Silence was not an intended virtue in and of itself; it was a means leading to unceasing prayer. Some people train themselves on silence for the sole intension of silence as a virtue. No, this should only be a means for the mind to become preoccupied with God. Therefore, when St. Isaac said, "Know that every loquacious man is inwardly empty,"[21] he meant void of unceasing prayer. For the sake of unceasing prayer the Fathers lived in the wildernesses and wastelands; they ventured into the inner desert in order to be isolated for God. For the sake of unceasing prayer they safeguarded the senses; there is a virtue called guarding the senses. The senses gather thoughts:

---

20 (Thornton and S 1998), 128; (Ramfos 2000), 99.
21 St. Isaac the Syrian (Miller 1984), 307.

what they see they think of, what they hear they think of, and likewise all that enters through the other senses; the senses are the doors to the thoughts. In order to arrive at peace of mind you need to control your senses; the goal behind peace of mind is reflecting on God.

Most monastic perusal was for the sake of unceasing prayer; reading also brings about thoughts, therefore the monastic chose readings that aided in prayer, or ones that facilitated fervor in prayer. Here we realize that not all readings are beneficial to a monastic whose goal is unity with God. One read until the emotions were moved towards God, and then one turned to prayer and stopped reading.

Unceasing Prayer Is an Expression of Love and Commitment to God

When you love someone, you often think of that person; when you love God, you think of Him often and are very preoccupied with Him. One who does not pray much does not love God much; the more a person loves God the more prayer towards God increases. It is an expression. If we say solitude and silence are means to aid prayer, we also say that prayer is an expression of our love for God.

The stories of monks in prayer are vast, you probably all know them very well; when we recall them, it is simply to feel their effect on us. Some examples include: St. Arsenius, who spent the entire night in prayer facing east, with the sun behind him, and continued in prayer until the sun rose before him once again;[22] St. Bishoy, who kept vigil all night in prayer and tied his hair lest he fall asleep;[23] St. Macarius the Alexandrian, who crucified his mind in God, telling it, "You have before you God and all His angels, remain in this sphere and do not leave,"[24] and he remained in this exercise for four days; and the saints who prayed unceasingly while working, to whom prayer was (as one of the saints expressed

---

22   (Ward, Desert Fathers 2003), 131.
23   (Colobos 1983), 167.
24   Cf. (Behr 2004), 148.

it) "the inhaled and exhaled breath."[25] To the saints prayer was in length, duration, depth, and nature. They did not simply spend a long time in prayer, but their prayers were full of fervor, reverence, humility, collected thoughts, love, tears, understanding, meditation, and humility of heart. It was prayer that often leads to visions or rapture in God, prayer that is able to perform miracles, and prayer that is able to open the gates of heaven.

Prayer is the Specialty of Monastics

If each secular person specializes in mastering a specific profession, a monastic specializes in mastering the profession of prayer. If one is intelligent, intelligence is vast in the world; a person seeking intelligence could find it in various places. People do not come to the monastic for intelligence. Also knowledge, many seculars are scholars who have various types of knowledge; one coming to a monastic comes for something else, not simply for the sake of knowledge, unless it is the knowledge of loving God and knowledge of His ways. People have an impression that monastics are like angels who have a relationship with God, whose prayer is acceptable before God. This is what people expect from monastics. If they find monastics not praying unceasingly they might be offended.

As a monastic prays, the prayer purifies, cleanses, and sanctifies the mind. It also purifies the heart. What you hear, read, or think leaves an impression in you; the state of your thoughts is also the state of your heart. If your thoughts bathe in the world, your heart will move in the world; if your thoughts bathe in sin, your heart will move in sin; if your thoughts are bound to God, your heart will also be bound to God. The heart and the mind go hand in hand. The more your mind attends to prayer the less opportunity it has to think of other matters.

If you decrease, diminish, refrain from, or feel languor

---

25   (Budge, The Paradise of the Holy Fathers 2008) Vol II, 342; (Payne 1982), 270; (Ward, Desert Fathers 2003), 158.

from prayer, then you provide an opportunity for evil thoughts to cling to you, or you provide an opportunity for the demons to toy with you as they will find the house "adorned, furnished,"[26] and prepared for any devil to dwell. For this reason, many spiritual fathers treated spiritual problems with prayer. The more a person prays, the more the mind clings to God; when the mind clings to God you are not free to think of sin, think of others, or think of any problems, because your mind is preoccupied with God. You know the story of St. John the Short, whose mind was continually preoccupied with God to the point that when the camel driver came seeking his basket weaving he was too absent-minded to consider it, and so he kept repeating, "Weaving—camel; weaving—camel,"[27] in order to remind himself. The further one's mind clings to God, the more one is unavailable to think of anything else, therefore many of the problems vanish, many of the sins disappear, evil thoughts fade away, worldly thoughts disperse, and people's problems fizzle; one is inaccessible. If you are praying, could the devil war against you with the sins of anger, vengeance, or condemning others? If the devil knocks on the door of your heart, he would find you busy. They say the lazy mind is a laboratory for the devil. Prayer is a remedy to evil thoughts and a purifier of hearts.

Prayer is Linked to the Life of Repentance

St. Isaac says, "Whoever thinks that there is any other door to repentance other than prayer is deceived by the devils."[28] This is double-sided: on the one side, prayer preoccupies the mind with God (one whose mind is preoccupied with God is not free to sin, but is prepared to repent); on the other side (which is not inferior, but rather superior) through prayer, you receive divine support, and divine support aids you to repentance.

In this context, prayer provides a virtue which we could call timidity of mind; the mind grows shy to think of something bad when it was just praying, too shy to think of a sin when

26   Cf. Mt 12:44
27   Saint John the Short (Ward, Sayings 1984), 92.
28   Cf. (Allchin 1990), 23.

it was just speaking with God; this is similar to a person who is ashamed to sin immediately after taking communion. Not praying (or abandoning prayer) provides an opportunity for distancing from God, so that, when the mind sins it is not timid because it has forgotten God completely, it has been too long since it remembered God. However, one who is praying keeps God in view: "I have set the Lord always before me."[29] Could you speak to Him just now and shortly betray Him? That would be unreasonable; therefore, the life of prayer leads to the life of purity, and the life of repentance.

Furthermore, prayer teaches us all the virtues. Believe me, if we meditated on the words of our prayers, for example the words in the Horologion (Agpeya), we would find all the various virtues contained within; you would find the entire spiritual road mapped out. Is it only the Horologion prayers? If you take the Lord's Prayer, you would find a long spiritual road open before you; each expression opens a spiritual opportunity. Prayer leads to meditation and meditation leads to prayer; prayer and meditation together lead to the life of virtue with all its details, what remains is implementation. It is sufficient for you in prayer to say, "Show me Your ways, O Lord; teach me Your paths.... Cause me to know the way in which I should walk."[30] In prayer God becomes your life-companion, therefore, unceasing prayer gives partnership, companionship, fellowship with God, and standing before the Divine presence. Sometimes, with interrupted prayers a person builds and demolishes: one builds spirituality during prayer, but during the long absence from prayer, what was built is demolished; therefore, the person continues to build and demolish without stability.

A monastic enters the monastic rite in order to learn how to sit with God, how to enjoy divine fellowship, and how to speak with God night and day, to the point that the effect of prayer appears even in dreams. In adhering to prayer, the world seems strange to the monastic, and returning to prayer feels like returning to the natural state. There is an amazing word said by St. Barsanuphius. They asked him, "What is

---

29   Ps 16:8
30   Ps 25:4; 143:8

unceasing prayer," to which he responded, "It is death to the world."[31] The heart of someone in continual prayer has no world in it; this is true death to the world. True death to the world is unceasing prayer, because prayer does not provide an opportunity for attachment to the world. Do they not say that monasticism is "Release from all, bondage to the One?"[32] When you unite with the One in unceasing prayer, you release from all because it is unreasonable to be united with everyone while you are praying, not even united with some, or else your prayer would contain distracting thoughts. Unceasing prayer without distractions is death to the world, because distraction is returning to the world once again.

How to Attain to Unceasing Prayer

Lest someone asks, "How many are the stories of the saints on unceasing prayer, and how many are the sayings of the fathers on unceasing prayer, but how could we attain it?" You would not attain it with one leap, but begin on the road and grow in it. What does this mean? My first advice: do not assume as a monastic that the seven prayers in the Horologion are your entire prayer canon, because these seven prayers are required of all secular Christians, those who work in the world, and likewise married persons. The first person who prayed these seven prayers was married: David the Prophet, who said, "Seven times a day I praise You, because of Your righteous judgments."[33] All Christians have the Horologion prayers, but monastics have unceasing prayer. Set your mind to organize for yourself a prayer program stronger, broader, and greater than the Horologion prayers by use of memorized prayers and prayers from your heart. Memorized prayers could include other psalms (not found in the Horologion), the prayers of saints (they are plenty), the many praises (the type we say on Apocalypses—they also are many and are written in books), and there are other prayers of the saintly Fathers from which one is able to read and chose what is needed, to learn prayer.

---

31 (Spidlik 1994), 363.

32 St. Isaac the Syrian (Miller 1984), 411.

33 Ps 119:164

Also, pray during your free time as much as you could, blend each work (any spiritual work or any work in the monastery) with prayer, and break up your time with prayers whenever the opportunity permits. Do not allow a long period of time to pass while you are away from prayer, even if by short repeated prayers, even if by lifting up your heart to God from time to time by any sentence (no matter how short). What is important is not to forget prayer, but to set it before you, always lifting up your heart.

Here I want to place before you two verses from the Holy Bible: we "always ought to pray and not lose heart,"[34] and, "pray without ceasing."[35] If these commandments were given to all Christians, then how much more were they for monastics! Who of us fulfills these two commandments? If you realize this, then do not boast in vain if you pray all your psalms and all the Horologion prayers, but tell yourself, "The program is very long before me, I am required to pray at all times, unceasingly." This suffices for now, so that we may give you an opportunity to pray.

Glory be to God forever. Amen.

---

34   Lk 18:1
35   1 Thess 5:17

THE DIFFERENCE BETWEEN MONASTIC LIFE AND SECULAR LIFE

In the Name of the Father, the Son, and the Holy Spirit,
One God. Amen.

Garrulity

Talkativeness is encouraged in the world, while in monasticism taciturnity is necessary. There is a disease called garrulity (talkativeness). Let us learn the reasons, problems, and treatments for this disease. Talking overmuch never suits monasticism, especially destructive conversations with which one person sits with a friend and completely demolishes that person. This could be by presenting thoughts that were not there; unknown news; doubts that are difficult to remove; or by introducing to the mind a sort of grumbling, protest, or internal rebellion, and leaving that person in this troubled condition, without supplying an exit.

Conversations that waste time do not suit monasticism. The time you spend in conversations, you could have spent in something beneficial, with which to build yourself or others. Alas, time is wasted in conversations, and this is a disease. The lives of secular people are full of conversations. If you sat next to a person and remained silent, one would blame you, "Why don't you speak, are you upset? Are we at a funeral?" As for monasticism, if converse is not edifying, it is destructive. If it does not destroy the soul, it at least destroys time.

Examples of Serious Monastics

Some monastics have built their lives in very short periods. Such examples are Sts. Maximus and Dometius who, in a very few years reached the peak, and their prayers were as tongues of fire rising up to heaven. This is while the beard of one of them had not yet fully grown; they were still youth. Another example is Misael the Anchorite who was about seventeen years old. Did he have time to talk? He lived a serious life of ceaseless spiritual work which did not allow opportunity for speech, relationships with others, or permitting them to establish freedom of speech. This is someone who is preoccupied with his salvation; he does not have time to talk, or to waste time. Also, St. Mina was martyred at the age of twenty-three. When did he become a monk? When did he become a monastic leader? When did he receive the gift of healing? When did he fill the world with miracles? And, when was he martyred? All in this short time! He was engaged in constant serious work. He had no time to waste in talking with others, neither in destroying nor in building. What do I mean by neither in destroying nor in building? Take for example, St. Arsenius, if he spoke with others, he would build them by his speech. Could not one to whom Pope Theophilus came seeking a beneficial word build others! This is someone with whom the saints desired to sit. Once St. Macarius the Alexandrian asked him, "Why do you flee from us father," to which St. Arsenius responded, "God knows that I love you, but I cannot be with God and with men."[36] This is someone seeking the salvation of his soul. On the contrary, two people may sit together and each one demolishes the other, pulling the other downward, and filling the other with words which might lead to thoughts that are unsettling. Why this waste! This is a disease called garrulity.

---

36   (Thornton and S 1998), 128.

Appreciating the Value of Time

St. Isaac the Syrian says, "Know that every loquacious man is inwardly empty,"[37] On the inside there is no prayer, meditation, spiritual work, preoccupation with God, or compunction, therefore the tongue is free to chatter. The talkative person does not appreciate the value of time, and has nothing of more importance or benefit with which to be preoccupied than talking. Garrulity wastes a person's spiritual work, prayers, relationship with God, and even intellectual growth. If you knew the value of time you would build yourself, read, be filled by the sayings of the fathers, be filled with knowledge, be filled with stories of the saints, be filled with books on the spiritual life, read in the Bible, or memorize verses. You would become a treasury of knowledge from abundant reading. It was said that Origen rented libraries and spent nights in them in order to read. St. Athanasius authored two books while not yet age twenty: *Treatise Contra Gentes*, and *On the Incarnation of the Word*; these are among the greatest books. He reasoned at the Council of Nicea while still a young deacon. This is because he was filled with knowledge. His time was valuable; he benefited from each moment. One who would ask you, "Would I sit and chat with a person for an hour? I would have read a book or several manuscripts in that hour. I would have been filled in that hour."

The one who talks only empties, is never filled, and most of those who empty are not peddling anything of value. At times one person's concerns and problems are above tolerance, and so pours them into another's ear, meanwhile the other person might have been naive, not knowing any concerns or problems. Certainly, this person hears the issue from one side. If you ask each one of them, "What have you benefited?" the response would be, "Nothing," "How have you been harmed?" "Plenty!" Believe me, what a person hears in a moment might take days, months, or even years to forget, and perhaps it will be impossible to forget.

---

37   St. Isaac the Syrian (Miller 1984), 307.

The Difference Between Monastic Life and Secular Life

That saint who repeatedly circled around his cell dusting out his ears before entering was very wise; he said, "I was sitting with people and heard a discussion, and the sound of this discussion remains in my ears, so I decided to empty them before the discussion comes with me into the cell."[38] How wonderful is the word of Abba Or to his disciple, "Take care not to introduce an alien word into this cell!"[39] What is the meaning of an alien word? It is a word alien to the monastic life, alien to spiritual benefit, a word that does not build. This is why we said there is a vast difference between monastic life and secular life. To the laity, one fluent in speech and converse (is able to take the helm of the conversation and move from one topic to another, and fill the listeners with words) is considered a sociable person; monasticism is not this way. One who fills the listeners with words wastes their time, unless they are meditating on the words of God in a way that builds the soul. Such was St. Macarius. When he sat to speak with his children they all wept, and he also wept until his beard was wet.

Garrulity is a disease. It is a craving for stories and spreading news. To the laity news and stories are good; they buy the newspapers and watch television for the news. However, news does not benefit the monastery; this is not its job (not world news, or Church community news, nor even monastic news are beneficial). A monastic is self-contained. What does one on whom they prayed the burial prayer have to do with news?

If you keep to yourself, you might find another come to ask, "Oh, haven't you heard?" and begins to relate the news, but only the details one wants to relay of the news. News brings thoughts, and thoughts scatter prayers, meditation, time, and oftentimes even disturbs the love towards others. See what Job told his friends: "Oh, that you would be silent, and it would be your wisdom!"[40] You might answer: "We know this verse." It is not important that you know it, it is

---

38 Saint John the Short Cf. (Ward, Sayings 1984), 91.

39 (Ramfos 2000), 28.

40 Job 13:5

more important for you to apply it. Eve not only memorized, but indeed with precision. The serpent came to her saying, "Has God indeed said, 'You shall not eat of every tree of the garden?' And the woman said to the serpent, 'We may eat the fruit of the trees of the garden; but of the fruit of the tree which is in the midst of the garden, God has said, "You shall not eat it, nor shall you touch it, lest you die."'"[41] This is utmost precision, yet at this same encounter she both touched and ate, and gave to another. Memorizing verses is easy, what is important is fulfilling them. Some people memorize verses in order to apply them to others, not to apply them to themselves.

Here I want to ask you a candid clear question: "Does every time you sit to speak with a friend in the monastery build you spiritually?" If it does not build you spiritually, then you are better off without. I remember how at the beginning of my monastic life this trial came to me in another form. One time I was in seclusion in my cell, I only emerged at the end of the week to pray. I was away from the news and thoughts, yet simultaneously I maintained my responsibilities in the monastery printing press while in seclusion. Someone who was unable to meet me or speak with me because I am in seclusion would knock saying, "Father Anthony, there is an issue we need you to pray for, because Father so-and-so is... Please remember him in your prayers," and in the name of prayer I learned the monastery news. If four or five prayer requests come in this fashion, then one is living in the heart of the monastery, and certainly not in seclusion. Even if he had not mentioned the details and only asked me to pray, my thoughts would have started to play: "What happened to so-and-so that he needs me to pray for him? What should I say Lord? Is he in trouble? Let me pass by his cell to see how he is doing."

Do you think that when the devil wants to waste your time he will tell you, as secular people, "Let's go to the movies"? Not at all! He wastes your time in very pleasant ways: a spiritual conversation with one of the saints who have died to the world could waste your whole night. And, if you try to

41   Gen 3:1–3

pray your psalms after this conversation, you find that your psalms have drifted into what your friend was saying. Where are the psalms? The psalms have dispersed; they have entered into the thoughts and news of so-and-so did, and this-and-that happened, and this one was upset ... and your psalms are gone. If this person befriends you and comes by every night, then "God help you!" As St. Isaac says, "If one of these comes by, with all humility offer him a prostration and ask him to forgive you because you have not completed your psalms. Invite him to pray with you, and pray your psalms with him."[42] Surely, this visitor had not come to pray the psalms; once you mention the psalms the visit will end. If you object, saying "but this could hurt a person's feelings, and in monasticism one does not hurt another's feelings." If it is of this kind only, then it is beneficial for both of you. At least you have reminded your visitor of the psalms, and it helps you complete your canon. Besides, you said nothing wrong; you apologized for not completing your psalms, and wanted to complete them with this person. This is why when the brethren were coming out of church, St. Macarius said "'flee, my brothers.' One of the old men asked him, 'Where could we flee to beyond this desert?' He put his finger on his lips and said, 'Flee that.'"[43]

The Virtue of Silence

Seculars would say, "This person's speech is interesting," but in monasticism they say, "This person's silence is consoling." In the world they say, "We learn from this person's speech," but in monasticism they say, "We learn from this person's silence." This is why I told you that secular virtues are different from monastic virtues. This does not prevent an occasional, gentle, comforting, blessed, knowledgeable, or spiritual word, but, as for the words with which you demolish your friend's spirituality: God will require that soul from you on the Last Day. Is this too difficult for you to hear? He will

---

42   Cf. (Miller 1984), 108.
43   (Ward, Sayings 1984), 131.

tell you, "This person spent many months gathering wheat into the barn, and in one mindless moment you burned it."

Prevention or Treatment

Garrulity is one of the dangerous diseases for which a monastic needs to take preventive measures or treatment measures. For preventive measures you would find that either you will need to live alone, or you will choose your friends from those whom you feel you are not harmed spiritually. Either remain alone, or give closed-ended answers. If a person tries to start a conversation, give closed-ended responses that would end the conversation, such as, "God will do what is good. God will arrange everything," adding nothing more, and, as *The Paradise of the Holy Fathers* said, "When the brother saw that he possessed not freedom of speech with the old man, he ... departed."[44] On the contrary, if one says, "Such-and-such happened," to which you respond, "Oh, and what else? And then what?" then you are opening up. One person might say, "So-and-so did this-and-that," to which another responds, "You just reminded me of something else he did," and they take turns discussing this person. One either uses closed-ended responses: "God willing. May God do what is right. God willing this will end well. Thank God," or remains silent. One might ask you, "Are you paying attention?" to which you respond, "Yes, I am." If you are able to go off on a tangent with the topic, that is great, but if you are unable to stray on the outside you could at least stray on the inside. If you are unable to change the subject, you could stray onto another subject internally while the person is speaking, like the one who repeated, "Weaving—camel; weaving—camel,"[45] for example, but not using his exact method. Think of anything else so that the conversation does not take root. There is another option: you could say, "You just reminded me of something," and drift from one subject to another, until you reach elsewhere. This is a mode of treatment. I ask God to

---

44   (Budge, The Paradise of the Holy Fathers 2008) Vol II, 14–15 {21}.
45   Saint John the Short (Ward, Sayings 1984), 92.

sanctify the tongues and ears of monks and nuns. This could not happen unless God sanctifies their hearts and emotions, and continually reminds them of the purpose for which they left on the day of their monasticism.

What is called "news" in the world is called "unsettlement" in the monastery. You would often find this word in *The Paradise of the Holy Fathers*; in monastic books it is called community unsettlement. News, thoughts, chatter, and such are all community unsettlement.

The Relationship Between Work and Prayer

When people come to eat baked bread, receive raised agricultural produce, eat a meal, or take handiwork from the monastery, one of the blessings they receive is that all these were done with prayer. They expect that the baker baked with prayers; the cook cooked while praying; the farmer planted while praying; and anyone performing any work for the monastery did it while praying. We should meet their expectations that we were praying, praising, chanting, reading spiritual material, and spending spiritual times. Ask yourself, "Is my mind thus occupied in every work I perform?" or is it simply too much chatter: bread with chatter, meals with chatter, planting with chatter, and all work with chatter? And who knows what kind of chatter. If people knew this, they would refuse to eat anything from the monastery. Oh, that we would not forget ourselves.

Secular people would say, "Have you met so-and-so? What an amazing character! You could spend two or three hours with this person and not feel it, time flies by as if a moment." In monasticism, if two or three hours flew by as if a moment, that would be a monastic catastrophe. Is this person able to waste your time in chatter? Delightful! This is why I told you that the standards of monasticism are different from the laity. We need to attend to utilizing our time wisely: to build ourselves, build others, or offer a good service to the monastery, and at the same time not waste our spirituality.

Death to the World

What is the significance of praying the funeral prayer on the person? Some people think that this prayer is only prayed on the white gown, so that it turns black, and the white gown dies. No, my beloved, the funeral prayer is prayed over your entire old personality, except the spirituality. Thus, you find yourself of a different make, having different thoughts than those of the world.

Long ago, before monasticism, a person might have spent all the time in service. Once one entered monasticism ... "What service?" "What about the tens of people who benefited from you?" "No, now I have come to benefit from people, not for people to benefit from me." One who was a teacher before monasticism, comes to monasticism to be a student who wants to benefit, wants to take in something beneficial for salvation. On the contrary, one who enters monasticism wanting to teach everyone and distribute wisdom on every passerby—one learns from his intelligence, one benefits from his knowledge, one benefits from his wisdom, one benefits from his experience, one benefits from his past, one benefits from his present, one benefits from his speech, one benefits from his silence!—No, this will never do! Before monasticism you were a renowned servant, yet you come to monasticism saying, "I've begun the life of discipleship. I want to become a disciple to all and benefit from each person, just as the saints became disciples."

St. Anthony benefited from a woman who was not ashamed to uncover herself in front of a man. She spoke the statement, but he said "this is God's voice," and benefited from her. St. Macarius benefited from a young cowherd. St. Moses the Black benefited from Zechariah the youth. Everyone wants to benefit, wanting to hear a word of benefit, not wanting to distribute information. You come to monasticism and forget that you had any information. Believe me, even the spiritual information that we had before monasticism, we found that when we entered monasticism it took on a new meaning, different from the first one, principles of monasticism, its spirituality, the sayings of the fathers, and their depth.

Struggling and Spiritual Growth

Here I will ask a candid question. Each one sit with yourself and ask the following: how many years have I spent in the monastery? How have I struggled for my spiritual growth during this period? What are the manifestations of this growth? How is it manifest in knowledge, in behavior, in changing life for the better, and in gaining monastic virtues? Perhaps these many questions will perplex you. Let us ask one simple question, easy to memorize. They say monastics are earthly angels, so, what steps have you taken in order to become an earthly angel? What is the distance between you and an angel? An even simpler question: have you been freed from the sins that you had in the world, are you the same, or have you entered into new sins that were not there before? Where are you right now? Misael the Anchorite, in three or four years became an anchorite, and you, how many years have passed by you, and have you become an anchorite, or even a monastic, or an angel? What have you become during this period? Or, do you need to begin again?

We are celebrating the monasticism of two new monks today. Oh, that each person would say the following expression: "I wish to be monasticised like them." Do not say, "I've become a monastic and an elder," say, "I wish I could become a monastic." Do not think this is my own expression. When St. Macarius saw two anchorites in the inner wilderness, he returned to tell his disciples, "I have not yet become a monk,, but I have seen monks."[46] A similar feeling was within St. Anthony when he saw St. Paul. Here, ask yourself what spiritual growth you have gained since you entered monasticism; what spiritual growth you have gained since you entered these black clothes (perhaps entered monasticism is too big a phrase). The saying of the Spiritual Elder is stern: "How long will you console yourself with dressing in black?"[47] Once you had put on the black cloth, you thought you had become a monastic!

---

46   (Vivian, Saint Macarius the Spiritbearer: Coptic Texts Relating to Saint Macarius the Great 2004), 67.

47   The Spiritual Elder John Saba. Cf. (Hansbury 2006), 76.

Monasticism is an internal process, inside the heart, inside the life, in the depth of the person; it works on the inside. It is never an external ritual.

I want to tell you something else, when you read St. John Climacus, you will find thirty steps of monasticism, steps of spirituality. Read them and see how many steps you have climbed: Exile (death to the world), have you fulfilled it; Detachment, have you completed it (we are still in the first steps). Have you been able to complete the monastic virtues: asceticism, renunciation, detachment, exile, obedience, and the rest of the virtues you read of in *The Paradise* and *The Sayings of the Fathers*, or are you still at the beginning of the path?

Self Evaluation

Monasticism needs you to be very honest with yourself, not ever justifying yourself or giving yourself excuses, but you reveal yourself before yourself completely, asking, "Now what? How far have we reached? And how far will we reach?" This is what Sts. Sisoes and Arsenius did. Continually examine yourself: "What have I done in monasticism? What have I taken from monasticism? And what is left for me?" Don't become oblivious! One day leading you to another, and one night handing you over to another, the years pass by and you are passing along with them, taking nothing out of monasticism. And if someone who knew you in the world saw you now, that person would see the same person, perhaps the same glances, the same tone, the same frown, the same temper, the same over-sensitivity, the same overreaction, and the same aggression. If this is the same person, then who died? "No one died; it was only a ritualistic prayer we said simply for consolation, so that he feels that he really died." Believe me, these things will never get us anywhere. My brethren, monasticism is not a new name we take, or new clothes we wear, it is not simply a cowl and girdle, it is not a new image. Monasticism is life, life even for those who have not taken the image, cloth, or name. You will ask me, who has not taken the image, cloth, or name. I answer you with someone like St. Paul. What did he take? Who prayed monastic prayer over him? Who dressed him in a cowl or girdle? He did not even dress in black, he dressed in palm leaves, yet he was more profound than all monks, and before him was abased the self-esteem of St. Anthony, the father of all monks; he saw himself as nothing when he saw St. Paul. St. Paul called St. Anthony "son," and St. Anthony called him, "father." Is it a matter of dress, or image? No. It is life. Death to the world begins in the heart from within. The first funeral prayer that they pray over you, your will has to pray over the lusts of the world that are in your heart. You have to die internally to the world and all that is in it, detach from everything, die to your old self, and take on a new name from God Himself, who blesses you and gives you a different life. The monastics of the monastery feel this and so they officially sanction it. The monastics are not the ones who make you die to the world; death to the world is something inside your heart. If they pray one hundred funeral prayers but you have not died internally, then are we fooling each other? Nothing has happened. It is an internal process.

The monastic is a blessing to any place he or she comes. We feel that the dedication of this person is a blessing to the monastery, that the dedication date is a feast for the monastery, and that this person's presence among us is the presence of a leader, an ideal, a living spiritual standard, a visible model of the life of virtue, and the presence of a person who has a relationship with God, to whom we resort whenever we want to use this relationship. Monasticism in not simply clothes and rituals. Oh, that each one of you would examine yourself, asking, "Have I truly become a monastic or not? Is it on the inside, or is it simply external monasticism? Genuinely or simply ritually? As life or simply a name and dress? What exactly has happened to me? Am I, in my life inside the monastery, treating all the events that I encounter in a monastic manner, or like all secular people, and like my old personality? What exactly has happened to me?" Let us be very honest with ourselves, because honesty is what is beneficial; it gives a person an opportunity to review the path and correct what needs correction.

Monasticism is not simply a change of life, but it is growth in this change, until a person reaches monastic perfection—the life of perfection. If monasticism is a life of prayer, are you growing in the life of prayer? If monasticism is a life of tranquility and stillness, have you grasped tranquility and stillness and are you continually growing in them? If monasticism is a life of purity and holiness, have you begun the way of purity and holiness and are you growing in them, or have you not yet begun the life of repentance? If monasticism is a life of renunciation (of the world and all that is therein as vain) and asceticism, have you entered the life of renunciation, asceticism, detachment, and the war with the desires (whatever they may be), or not yet? Do not fool yourself. Be honest with yourself! You could defend yourself before any person, but you could not defend yourself before yourself, "For what man knows the things of a man except the spirit of the man which is in him?"[48] You know yourself very well. You could give an altered impression to others, but you could not give an altered impression to yourself (unless you are fooling yourself, but this is something we do not look forward to).

Conclusion

To sum up, let us have a very serious session with ourselves, in order to evaluate our monastic life with precision, and to correct any of our monastic behaviors that need correction. May God attend this session, or may it be in His presence. "He who searches the minds and hearts"[49] knows what is in our depth, and may He help us with His grace to walk as is fitting.

To Him be glory from now and forever. Amen.

---

48   1 Cor 2:11
49   Rev 2:23

THE SWITCH TO THE MONASTIC PERSONALITY

In the Name of the Father, the Son, and the Holy Spirit, One God. Amen.

I would like to speak with you about an important issue in monasticism: the change in personality. One who becomes a monastic does not simply change the clothes (such that they become black), image, name, or dwelling place, but there must be an internal change in the personality.

Exchanging the Lay Personality for the Monastic Personality

Monastic virtues have their own special standards, which are above and beyond general Christian virtues. By general Christian virtues, I mean virtues such as a good reputation, a sanctified heart, and wise decision-making. There are certain monastic virtues, without which a monastic would not be complete in the monastic life. Such virtues include humility, self-denial, absolute death to the world, silence, stillness, non-possessiveness, contrition, and inner peace. All of these are essential to a monastic. Some lay persons have these virtues, and therefore, we are put to shame if they surpass monks on the monastic pathway.

In monastic life, one should conduct a self-examination saying: "Have I commenced on the way or not? Do I still have the same lay image and traits, or have they changed? Would someone who sees me now, see the same old person, only wearing different clothes? Or would that person say that I am a completely changed person from before?" Simply living in a monastery is not monasticism; monasticism is a change of the heart—it is internal. The heart must die to everything; no desire should attract it—this is the change. Otherwise, what is the meaning of the funeral prayers that are prayed over the person? Is it simply a ritual, or is it work inside the heart? As a monastic you must monitor yourself, and ask, "Has monasticism changed anything within me, or not? Was the change for the better, or have I started to fall into new sins that I did not use to fall into before monasticism? Is my monasticism a search for the upright spiritual work, or is it an imitation of people? Is it out of jealousy? Is it words read from a book while the reality of the heart is something completely different?"

You became nuns (or monks) a few months ago; in these months did you feel that you were changing yourselves? The wise one would monitor her mistakes, and struggle against them; but to leave yourself to roam according to your own passions is not monasticism. As one of the fathers said, "I know of no fall that happens to a monk that does not come from trusting his own judgment."[50] How can you subdue your own will, and seek and follow through with guidance? When will you be able to keep yourself from grumbling against instructions given you, or keep from assuming yourself wiser than your spiritual guide? Whenever a person is troubled in monasticism, that person thinks of changing external conditions in order to find rest, but the sound method is to change the state of the heart internally. What does this mean? It means that one who is troubled in monasticism might claim: "If I change my work, then I will be fine. If I change my cell, I will be fine. If the person responsible is changed this would be better and I will find rest. If the behavior of father so-and-so changes, I will find rest." All of these are attempts to alter external circumstances rather than change the heart from within. How to manage under these conditions—this is when you decide to renew your heart.

---

50   Dorotheos of Gaza (Wheeler 1977), 126.

Repairing the Heart

We are continually speaking of reconciling people, altering our location and environment, and correcting organizations, but we do not speak of correcting ourselves. We do not change because our selves are beautiful and righteous in our own eyes, and we say, "I never make a mistake, it is their fault." When monastics do not think of changing themselves, this causes problems for them. One may remain in monasticism for thirty years in this very same condition: it is true that the black clothes are renewed and changed on the outside, but the personality remains the same as it was when it came out of the world. This is not a good state to be in. Why then did we change our names and assume the names of saints? We are given the names of saints in order to know that the secular personality has ceased. But if it remains, then where is monasticism? Each one of you must do three things: 1) make a comparison between her lay personality and her current personality, and see what has changed in it, and what needs changing; 2) recall the guidance that she was given but which she did not fulfill; and 3) recognize which sins hinder her advancement in the life of grace.

After we assess our condition, we must be serious about changing ourselves for the better, because Christ said, "I have come that they may have life, and that they may have it more abundantly."[51] Take, for example, one who while secular was over-sensitive and was moved or upset by every word or action, one who always wept and depressed those around her, another one who was accustomed to blaming others as a result of the slightest remark made to her, one who was jealous, another one who talked excessively, one who suspected the worst of people, or yet another who was proud; these are all internal characteristics, have they changed or not? Have they assumed a monastic image? Some people, upon learning of their mistakes (or their surroundings having reveal their mistakes to them) are troubled by them and decide to seclude themselves in the cell, thinking that this will turn them into

---

51 Jn 10:10

saints. This is not the case. Do you think that by secluding yourself in your cell you will become one of the saints? This same personality, with all its troubles, will reside inside your cell also. One may seclude herself in her cell with her pride, her anger, and her troubles, and when the appropriate time comes for her to exit her cell, she emerges from her cell, and all her mistakes come out with her. Thus, the matter is not one of secluding ourselves in our cells, but it is a matter of eliminating the mistakes from our hearts.

Mistakes are revealed to a person in one of two ways: 1) through self- examination, or 2) the self is revealed by others. Let us suppose you are unable to perceive your own shortcomings; and so your father confessor or guide tells you: "So-and-so, you have not been good concerning such-and-such point." Will you react in anger saying: "Oh, I'm not good? Now I know that you do not love me!" Does love mean patting a person on the back? No, love means revealing ones sins. Some people become upset when their mistakes are revealed, and if people are aware of this characteristic in you, then they might not speak honestly with you, and you will suffer loss and perish. Alternatively, they might be honest with you, and consequently you may lose your relationship with them. For example, one's guide may tell her: "You were wrong in this situation," so she replies saying: "Oh, I'm wrong? I see, so-and-so must have sat with you and filled your ears." This way this nun is accusing her guide of taking sides, and at the same time she is accusing the other person of gossiping. And so, new sins are added to the old sins; in this way one can never be corrected.

Concern About Nothing in the World but God Alone

The monastic who cares only for God is one who thinks of nothing except his or her eternity, not of life upon earth. All other cares pertain to earth, but God is specific to eternity. If your eternity is everything in front of your eyes, you will not care about anything on earth. In the monastery you may be concerned with your status, your position and work, your relationship with those in responsibility, and if you are better than others or if others are better than you; all of these are issues which pertain to the earth. Perhaps in the monastery you are at the end of the line, but with God you are at the front of the line. If you care about your eternity, none of these matters will concern you. As one of the saints said: "Most highly esteemed are the ones indifferent to the world, in whose hand it lays."[52] In order to be concerned for nothing except God alone, you must have a humble heart, because most troubles that affect a person in the world are caused by an exalted heart internally. In other words, you must think that "*my* honor, *my* personality, *my* rights, and *my* integrity" are all matters of pride. With every concern ask yourself, "What does this have to do with my salvation?" And you will come to realize that none of the issues that cause concern affect our salvation, as St. Paul says, "Who shall separate us from the love of Christ?"[53]

The Monk Is Blind, Mute, and Deaf

The idiom of being blind, mute, and deaf, means that a monk or a nun should not interfere in the affairs of others. In brief, one should say, "What have I to do with the others, what brought me into this?"[54] Even Christ said this by claiming, "Who made Me a judge or an arbitrator over you,"[55] although He certainly is the Judge of all. One should live in the monastery without interfering in anything; rather you should say, "I am seeking my own salvation and have no business in this matter. The one who is wrong is wrong, and the one who is correct is correct, but as for me, I mind my own business." You should not allow the mistakes of others to greatly affect you, you should not cause a commotion because of other people's mistakes, you should not spread gossip from one person to another, and you should not speak concerning the actions of people. Quite simply, the expression "blind, mute,

52 Saint Ephrem the Syrian (Beni-Suef Publication Committee 1977), 173.
53 Rom 8:35
54 (Ward, Wisdom 1997), 3.
55 Lk 12:14

and deaf" means, "What business is it of mine?" One might say that another's action will destroy the monastery. Yet, if the action is truly wrong, it will surely be revealed; you should not necessarily be the one who reveals it. It will be revealed on its own. If you place yourself as a watchdog over the actions of others, then, as the saying goes, you will have turned from a worshipper into a judge. Did you come to work as judges, or worshippers? Each one of us should say, "I will keep to myself. What business is it of mine? What brought me into all of these affairs?"

There is a nice narrative concerning Abba Poemen. It talks of two monks who were insulting each other, and although he saw them, Abba Poemen kept silent. They began to hit one another, but Abba Poemen still remained silent. Then one of his brothers asked him, "Do you not see that these two are fighting?" to which he responded, "They are brothers and are destined to reconcile." Then when they started to beat and injure each other, he asked him again, "Do you see them and are unwilling to move, while these are injuring each other," so Abba Poemen looked at him and said: "Brother, lay it to thy heart that I [Poemen] am not here."[56] This is what it means to be blind, mute, and deaf. The person who wishes to maintain peace of heart should say, "I will keep to myself, what business is it of mine?" One who is impelled, saying, "I am concerned for the safety of the monastery and with avenging the wronged," has abandoned concern for salvation, and has become concerned about the safety of the monastery and justifying the wronged. In other words, this one has entered into administration and politics, whilst forgetting salvation. The wronged will be avenged by God, the peace of the monastery will be protected by God, those commissioned have their own responsibilities, and each of you should keep to yourself. If you keep to yourself, you will be respected by all, loved by all, and trusted by all, and if you do intervene on any given occasion, your word will have a postive impact.

---

56   (Thornton and S 1998), 159.

Connecting with God While Overloaded with Work

If your work is for God, and you feel that it is for God's sake, then you should not be disturbed or unsettled. What would disturb you is if you feel that the only cord binding you to God is prayer. To comfort yourself you can say the following: "Lord, today I will reach you through prayer, and I thank You for giving me a chance to speak with You." And on another day you may say to Him: "Today I will reach You through obedience," and on yet another day: "Today I will reach You by serving others." You can also pray saying: "O Lord, obedience leads to You, service leads to You, loving people leads to You, and prayer leads to You." And in this way you will live with peace in your heart. If you feel that only prayer leads to God, and everything else is outside God, you will neither believe in work and its benefits, nor anything else, and this will disturb you. Say to yourself, "For God's sake I will work, for God's sake I will pray, and for God's sake I will love people." Do this and you will live happily in every condition. St. Paul says, "Were you called while a slave?"[57] You could still reach God. What if I was called while a slave (people could enslave me today), but I will still reach God while a slave. Do not let such things occupy your thoughts. God seeks internal purity of heart more than millions of prayers which emerge from a grumbling, angry, unsettled, and anxious heart.

Internal Calmness in a Life Full of Constant Problems

Leave all problems outside of your heart, not inside. If they are outside, they will not trouble you; if they enter, they will bother you. Do not take problems to heart, do not solve them with your nerves, and do not overstate their size or impact. View situations with simplicity and let them take their natural course. What disturbs and unsettles a person's calmness is not the problem, but it is a person's way of dealing with a situation. A person's viewpoint and method of dealing with situations are what cause a person to lose calmness.

---

57 1 Cor 7:21

Glory be to God forever. Amen.

MONASTICISM IS A LIFE OF STRUGGLE

In the Name of the Father, the Son, and the Holy Spirit,
One God. Amen.

The Life of Monasticism Is a Life of Struggle

A person beginning a virtuous life will certainly be exposed to the devil's envy. Once the monastic begins the life of virtue, they also begin. Negligent monastics do not need the devil to fight them, for they fight against themselves and the devils are not wearied by them. In one story, a beginner went to St. Bishoy saying, "I beseech your holiness to pray to God for me, the worthless one, for I am being severely assaulted by the demons." St. Bishoy prayed for him, and consequently, the devil appeared to St. Bishoy, saying, "Believe me, I did not yet know, if this beginner came into the desert. By no means have I bothered him, but he is being fought by his own carelessness. However, from now on let him prepare to taste my own dreaded temptations and attacks, which I have conceived to war against him."[58] Thus, the devils unleashed ferocious attacks against the elders and those laboring in the way of monasticism.

What Does the Expression "Laboring Monastic" Mean?

It means a monastic who labors spiritually, whether externally regarding the monastic canon, or internally within one's heart by keeping one's thoughts, one's heart, and one's desires away from the world while also preserving one's estrangement. One keeps the senses from wandering here and there, battling against thoughts which are the internal wars inside a person. A monastic that has not yet begun spiritual labor will, most

---

58 (Colobos 1983), 39–40.

likely, not be exposed to such warfare, or perhaps will be attacked by wars resembling the warfare from which seculars suffer.

When St. Paul the Simple was living with St. Anthony, he wanted to continue living under the shadow of St. Anthony's prayers. But, a time came when St. Anthony said to him, "Go live in a cave alone." He answered, "Father, I would like to stay with you." St. Anthony replied, "Behold, you are a monk, and henceforth you must live by yourself so that you may receive the temptations of devils."[59]

Who Is the Experienced Monastic?

An experienced monastic is not necessarily an elderly monastic, or a monastic who has spent many years in monasticism. However, this is a monastic who has entered into the diabolic warfare and has become acquainted with this warfare. Such a person has learned of their thoughts, is well aware of their trickery and traps, and knows how to resist them. Thus, St. Anthony said, "I saw the snares that the enemy spreads out over the world."[60]

The Devil is Very Patient

It is said in *The Paradise of the Holy Fathers* that the devil attacked a monk for a period of forty years in order to have him fall into a particular sin.[61] Satan does not give up, or become bored or wearied; and for the sake of one sin, he is willing to work for a long time, in lengthy, gradual steps until he spreads out his nets in order to overthrow the monastic and cause the monastic to fall into sin. This is similar to the story in which he caused the monk Jacob the Struggler to fall.[62] Every step leads to another, regardless of time, for time

59   (Budge, The Paradise of the Holy Fathers 2008) Vol 1, 127.
60   (Ward, Desert Fathers 2003), 2.
61   (Budge, The Paradise of the Holy Fathers 2008) Vol 2, 168; (Ward, Desert Fathers 2003), 48–49; (Ward, Sayings 1984), 97.
62   See El-Bustan (Bishop Mettaous 2005), 39.

is insignificant to Satan. There are swift strikes that achieve immediate results and there are strikes that achieve results after years, but the main point is that they do achieve results. Satan is very patient, crafty, and extremely intelligent. That is why the serpent is described in the Bible as "more cunning than any beast of the field."[63]

Satan is exceptionally clever and very knowledgeable, as St. Isaac said, "You are battling against a being that has seven thousand years of experience battling against man."[64] He has studied human nature very closely and has learned of the internal and external nature of the human soul. He also knows its weaknesses and of the ways in which to tempt it, overthrow it, and so forth. He can strike on the left or strike on the right according to the circumstances available to him, and according to the type of human soul that he encounters.

Who is the Greatest Psychologist Known to Mankind?

I will tell you, it is Satan, because he is the most skillful psychologist with the most experience concerning the human soul. He has examined thousands of human souls and many different types of people, and he knows how to deal with those who reject him. A person may reject Satan today but then run after him speedily two years later. Satan does not get bored, or say, "There is no hope in this person" simply because that person rejected him once. Satan does not lose hope in anyone, but rather, everyone is deemed susceptible to falling. Perhaps the most pleasant and comforting verse for Satan, and the one which gladdens his heart and is considered a crown upon his head, is the verse in the Holy Bible which says, "For all have sinned and fall short of the glory of God."[65] Also, "There is none who does good, no not one."[66] Obviously, this is the result of his efforts, experience, intelligence, and tricks.

Satan is an expert in the Holy Bible and its verses. Perhaps

63 Gen 3:1
64 Cf. (Miller 1984), 269.
65 Rom 3:23
66 Rom 3:12

if you ask me, "Who has memorized the Holy Bible more than anyone else?" I will tell you, "Satan," and he is capable of distorting Biblical verses in order to convey his personal convictions so that he may persuade people. Even at the temptation of our Lord Jesus Christ, he used verses from the Holy Bible, but of course with incorrect interpretations. Satan is talented in many areas, including music, poetry, philosophy, art, painting, sculpture, and all types of amusements. He is ready to teach anyone anything, accompanying one along the way, giving promises that he will not fulfill, and enticing one with those things one cannot obtain, for the Holy Bible says of him, "He is a liar and the father of it."[67]

Satan Seizes Opportunities to Do Battle

Sometimes, when Satan seeks to overthrow particular people and cause them to fall into a particular sin, he does not tempt them with that sin, but rather he uses numerous battles that lead to lukewarmness, laziness, materialism, and egotism to distance the person a little from the Bible, the psalms, meditation, thier father confessor, and the altar. After long preparations, Satan begins to fight that person; he prepares carefully and schemes a long time for the war. He does not carry out his assaults randomly, but plans for them. Satan may have a particular sin in mind in order to cause a person to fall, but it must first be preceded by another sin that will lead to it. He may want people to fall into fornication, so he tempts them using many devices involving relaxation, eating and drinking, laziness, leisure, the love of other things, and many things related to the company which they keep. And so, when the temptation comes, that person will be ready to accept it. With another person, Satan might strike with a sudden blow, such that you will not know your head from your toes.

Satan can also appear in the guise of an angel of light, or images of saints, speaking extraordinary spiritual words, offering contemplations and presenting sin in the guise of virtue. Therefore, concerning this matter, the Lord Jesus

---

67 Jn 8:44

Christ said, "Beware of false prophets who come to you in sheep's clothing, but inwardly they are ravenous wolves."[68] It means that sin is clothed in sheep's clothing so that it appears to be a virtue. Sometimes, the "right-sided blows" are of this kind; that is, they appear to be virtues.

Deception of the Devils

Suppose that Satan wants to have a monastic leave the monastery and have that monastic walk in the way of the world, or suppose that he wants to strike one physically, and so forth. Firstly, he will have you increase in prayers, in prostrations (metanoias), and in solitude, leading you to the extreme in bodily abstinence. Secondly, he will create conflict with the father confessor. For example, if the father confessor tells you, "No, my child, these are extreme ways, there is no need for them," Satan begins to make you doubt your father confessor. Doubting the father confessor is a widely known war of devils. After doubting, Satan can cause you to leave the father confessor, eventually leading that person to walk in extreme ways and to fall into pride. Following this, Satan will conjure up dreams and visions for you until you trust in them. Satan may then present you with misleading dialogues and other deceiving visions in order to draw you down to the place which he so desires. During this strike, Satan may cause you to fall into carnal sins. So, at first, it is not evident that the battle will result in such outcomes, nor do you ever think that such things will occur.

How Can One Combat the Devil's Warfare?

Whosoever studies diabolic warfare from the stories of the Fathers would encounter extraordinary things. The most effective way to combat the war of devils includes three factors: humility, prayer, and guidance. Prayer provides a person with strength from God; guidance reveals the work of the devil to

---

68 Mt 7:15

the father confessor who provides support through spiritual
fatherhood; and humility enables grace to draw near to the
person and deliver that person. It is rare for a person who
practices humility, guidance, and prayer to be defeated by the
devil. The devil's warfare also requires wisdom, experience,
and discernment; the Holy Bible mentions the "discerning
of spirits."[69] Therefore, a person can recognize the thoughts
which are from God, those which are from the devil, and
those which are from people, discerning between them all.
One of the greatest expressions about discerning such issues
was spoken by St. Paul when he said, "We are not ignorant of
his devices."[70] He also speaks of "those who by reason of use
have their senses exercised to discern both good and evil."[71]
Here, St. Paul is referring to trained spiritual senses that
understand satanic wars. St. Evagrius is one of the monastic
fathers, who, in his books on the diabolic warfare and their
thoughts, has spoken much about satanic wars and thoughts,
and the ways to resist them. One of the greatest aspects of St.
Evagrius' teachings is that he describes which Bible verse to
use to resist each thought from the devil.[72] So, every thought
can be refuted with a verse from the Bible. He said, "We do
not forget the devils that fight us but we rather respond to
them with verses from the Holy Scripture lest their unclean
thoughts stay with us."[73]

Some of Satan's Strategies for War

Among one of the devices of Satan is speed. He suggests
a thought and vigorously insists that people perform it
immediately. Why? So as not to give them the opportunity to
pray, expose their thoughts to the father confessor, receive
spiritual guidance, or take time to consider the matter and
think about it. St. Isaac says that when any thought comes to
you urging you to act upon it immediately, know with certainty

---

69 1 Cor 12:10
70 2 Cor 2:11
71 Heb 5:14
72 See (Brakke 2009).
73 Cf. (Corinth 1979–95), 29–71. (B. H. Vlachos 1995), 217.

that it is from the devil.[74] Our Lord does not like hastiness or speed, but He likes everything to be done carefully and calmly. As I told you, speed means that there will be no time for prayer, guidance, or thought about the matter in question; and this is what Satan likes.

In his wars, Satan works gradually; he deceives and he presents everything falsely and not as they are in reality. He is not embarrassed if his deception is discovered. He also incites a person to treat a particular sin with another, or cover up a sin with another sin until he leads a person into an endless and long series of sins which have no end. Satan is not content with the severity of the fall in which he has led a person, but rather, he will always try to drag that person further down until he leads that person into complete despair and the loss of hope in salvation. At this stage, that person becomes like a puppet in Satan's hands. Despair and losing all hope in salvation is that which the third Psalm refers to when it says, "Many are they who say of me, 'There is no help for him in God.'"[75] Meaning, Satan attempts to make sin a habit in humans or cause it to become a part of their nature. This is so that people will commit sin without thinking, perhaps even unintentionally, and without gaining any pleasure or profit from the sin. They sin, rather, because sin has become a spontaneous part of their nature.

Just as Satan has recruited soldiers from amongst the ranks of fallen angels, he also likes to recruit soldiers from amongst the race of humans. Satan employs this strategy so that not only do his human soldiers fall themselves, but they also cause others to fall with them. In turn, those who have been made to fall are converted into stumbling blocks in the way of other people. These human soldiers become assistants of the devil and he reigns over them. The most serious condition achieved by Satan is when he reigns over a person by seizing and possessing that person. Such people sometimes speak with voices unlike their own, perhaps in a language that is not their own, or provide information that is also not their own; they simply utter the thoughts of Satan

---

74   Cf. (Miller 1984), 309.
75   Ps 3:2

who dwells inside them. This condition is referred to as "subjected," meaning that the person becomes submissive to Satan, or enslaved by Satan and defeated by him.

Such conditions are obviously difficult, but what is more extraordinary, is that in the lives of the saints we read that some great saints were deceived by Satan. For example, Abba Galion the anchorite went out with the intention of becoming an anchorite as the result of a deception by Satan.[76] He was a solitary monk who, for decades, lived in his monastery without ever leaving it until he reached old age. In fact, he had not stepped outside of the monastery for over sixty years. Then Satan deceived him so that he would become an anchorite and caused him to leave the monastery immediately. He did not give him a chance to meet a spiritual father, using the same strategy of speed mentioned earlier.

Satan has even led some hermits and anchorites astray. St. Timothy the anchorite was deceived while he was an anchorite.[77] St. Jacob the solitary sinned and fell while he was a hermit who performed miracles. Satan has no regard for anyone; he does not say, "This person is an anchorite so I will respect that person," or "This person is a solitary"; he does not even respect a prophet. Satan caused David the prophet to fall into sin while he was a prophet, that is, the Lord's anointed. Satan can cause anyone to fall, and he even attempted to do battle against the Lord Jesus Christ. He had the audacity to tempt the Lord Jesus Christ Himself! And when did he try to tempt Him? After the glorious divine appearance on the Feast of Theophany, the day of His baptism, after Satan heard the divine voice, "This is my beloved Son, in Whom I am well pleased."[78] Nevertheless, Satan had no regard for this, and came to battle against the Lord. Therefore, never think, at any time, that you have reached a level that is above the warfare of the devils. Humans must continue to live in vigilance and fear all the days of their lives. The Holy Bible says, "Conduct yourselves throughout the time of your stay here in fear.... Work out your own salvation with fear and trembling.... Therefore let him who thinks he stands take

---

76   See (El-Soriany 1993), 118–121.

77   See (El-Soriany 1993), 143–145.

78   Mt 3:17

heed lest he fall," [79] like St. Bishoy and the woman who caused his disciple Isaac to fall.[80]

Let us be deeply ashamed of our sins and so say to the Lord, "If we are not holy, You sanctify us," and entreat Him in every prayer saying, "Purge me with hyssop, and I shall be clean; wash me, and I shall be whiter than snow."[81] Sanctify me.

Glory be to God forever. Amen.

---

79   1 Pet 1:17; Phil 2:12; 1 Cor 10:12

80   (Colobos 1983), 42–45.

81   Ps 51:7

CONTROLLING THE THOUGHTS DURING PRAYER

January 1992

In the Name of the Father, the Son, and the Holy Spirit,
One God. Amen.

Pure Prayer

I would like to speak with you now about controlling your thoughts during prayer. Thought control during prayer reaches its climax when prayer is void of distraction or drifting, which leads to what the fathers call pure prayer—pure of any extraneous thoughts. The fathers say that distraction-free prayer is not for beginners because distraction-free prayer requires great labor. Beginners fulfill many duties and encounter many persons, which could generate thoughts, and thus they might drift into these thoughts.

The fathers say that the senses are the doorway to the thoughts: what you see you might think of; what you hear you might think of; what you touch, smell, taste, etc. Therefore, controlling the thoughts requires controlling the senses; if the senses are active it is difficult to control the thoughts. The senses of the fathers in the wilderness found no new material—it was the same scene, same sand, same sky; there was no new image for them to ponder upon. They had grown accustomed to the scene, and so their senses became restrained. If you want to restrain your thoughts in prayer, then control your senses. Do not allow your senses to stray and then complain of drifting or being distracted.

This is what St. Isaac said: "How can they reach pure prayer while each day they are building and demolishing";[82]

---

82 Cf. (Nineveh 1995), 178.

each time a spiritual thought is built it is demolished by worldly or secular thoughts. Pure prayer needs you to be anchored in spiritual thoughts. It needs the life of solitude; they call the life of solitude the life of stillness (Hesychism). One who enters the life of solitude controls the thoughts and senses. This is not available to monastics living in community. Therefore, you would need to confine yourself to the cell, and yet, cell confinement needs a person who knows how "to sit in the cell."[83] St. Isaac says it is possible that "such a person spends a hundred years in his cell, and does not even learn how one should sit."[84] Training the senses is a necessary basis for staying in the cell.

Control Your Thoughts Continually

Be faithful in what is few and God will set you over what is much.[85] Be faithful in controlling your senses and controlling your thoughts outside prayer, and God will give you pure prayer. If you want to control your thoughts during prayer, control your thoughts before prayer.

Control your thoughts throughout the day. What does this mean? To begin with, do not take issues outside prayer into great depth, which makes them ingrained in your thoughts, and thus they wage war against you during prayer. If you have a responsibility in the monastery, let it carried out normally. If you stop at every detail and turn it into an issue, it will turn into a problem, and you will start thinking about it in depth. It will remain with you and will be rooted in you, and at the time of prayer it will come to mind. If one says a word to you, you could accept the word calmly, or you could think about it deeply: "Why did he say this? What did he mean? Did he mean to belittle me? Will I let this go? If I let it go he will become even bolder with me. I cannot keep quiet. Then what will I do?" Here you have allowed the word to affect you profoundly, and so it became deeply-rooted in you, and so at the time of prayer you recall it. Therefore, do not ponder

83 (Ward, Sayings 1984), 91.
84 (Hausherr 1990), 72.
85 Cf. Mt 25:21

daily events in depth; overlook them and allow them to pass by calmly. Only those thoughts which take root in your mind and heart will bother you.

Passing thoughts could never trouble you. Only the thought to which you open your gates and allow entry will trouble you. This is why we say in the psalm, "Praise the Lord, O Jerusalem! Praise your God, O Zion! For He has strengthened the bars of your gates; He has blessed your children within you."[86] This means that the gates of the thoughts are shut against thoughts of the adversary and [drifting], sealed against every lust and desire, and blessed are your children born to you of the Holy Spirit inside the heart. Progressively He has blessed your children within you, and passively he has strengthened the bars of your gates. If you turn every word into an issue or a problem, and turn the world upside down, then naturally when you come to pray you will find your mind full of harmful thoughts. Issues that you let to affect you in depth settle down inside you, and sometimes appear as thoughts, assumptions, and dreams, or they interfere with your prayer. This is because you have opened to them a door and had given them much thought.

This is why a person needs to be simple in life. Forgive me if I tell you that some people say that dealing with monastics is not easy; if one says a word to a secular person, that person might take it as a joke and so that person is considered an easygoing person, if it is said to a monastic, there might be an analysis: "What do you mean? Am I the type of person you would say this to?" Do not scrutinize every word or allow it to cause problems for you; take things lightly. Your responsibilities might overwhelm you greatly, and so you think about them deeply all the time. Take for example one who works in the garden, this one might sit to think, "Ok, we need to do this and that ... and if we do this we need workers..." and sits to think about what to do next, day and night, and when this person comes to pray, his responsibility will disturb his thoughts.

---

86 Ps 147:12–13

Death to the World

Here I remember a beautiful response given by St. Barsanuphius; when they asked him "What is pure prayer?" He answered, "Death to the world."[87] What is death to the world? If the world remains alive inside of you, then you will continue thinking about it, and prayer will not be pure, you will drift into it. Death to the world means you die to all worldly issues, therefore, no longer are there issues of great importance to occupy you during prayer. As long as something occupies you during prayer, then you have not yet died to that to which your thoughts drift; if you had died to it, it would not come to mind. To preserve calm, distraction-free prayer do not be occupied with your problems and the problems of others. This preoccupation makes you drift into thinking about these problems. Imagine that you do not have any problems, and, if you have problems, try not to occupy yourself with them. There are people who are occupied with problems regardless if they are, or are not, commissioned with responsibility. Keep your peace-of-heart; from peace-of-heart emerges pure prayer. If the peace-of-heart is lost, then what squanders this peace becomes the cause for mental distraction.

Avoid community turbulence, so that its issues, thoughts, and problems do not distract you. The monastic who dwells on community turbulence, with its news and problems, plucks of the tree of knowledge of good and evil every day, and vacillates between good and evil all their lives. Do not allow your mind to think of anything except that for which you will offer a which you will have to answer to before God on the Last Day.

Perhaps, upon entering monasticism you no longer continue living in the world, and yet the world continues to live inside of you; this could be a cause for distraction. The world might live inside you with all its news, thoughts, problems, and anxieties, or there might be cravings that continue to move your heart, and they are the cause of your mental distraction. I do not mean specifically a desire for marriage—

---

87 (Spidlik 1994), 363.

any desire, for example: a person might have a desire for a specific responsibility in the monastery, or a responsibility in the world; another might have a desire for personal dignity; a third might lose peace over the ranking in the monastic order. Did you leave the whole world to seek a rank? This interferes with prayer and the monastic becomes concerned: "How could they offer to so-and-so and not offer to me ... or to offer me less?" Thus, part of the world continues to live within you: some pride, some vainglory, some self-centeredness; this could affect you greatly during prayer, and renders each word's effect "powerful and effective."[88] Something remains alive within; it has not died.

Seek out the issues that revolted against the burial rite prayed over you on the day of your monasticism. Has everything within you died, or did something revolt and say, "No, I refuse to die!" and remained alive, causing you distraction at the time of prayer? Perhaps its consequences could cause distraction, therefore, control your thoughts before prayer, control your thoughts while carrying out your responsibilities, during your work, during your encounters, during your relationships, and also do not give worldly matters much thought.

Remedy Your Mind

Your mind must have constructive spiritual work. Set up a balance between the spiritual and the secular realm in your life. How much do your thoughts enter into the secular and how much into the spiritual? If the secular thoughts allowed entry are many, then you will be distracted during prayer, but if the spiritual are more, then, even if you drift you will do so in a spiritual matter, and this could be a type of prayer or meditation. Your mind is constantly working (there is no idle mind), and so, offer it material to chew on. If you find nothing to occupy it, you could look at this picture, the chandelier, the cup, or the wall. The brain will work on any material, so give it spiritual material to occupy it, and thereby, worldly thoughts will not be strong when they find the mind

---

88 (Christ 1989), NRSV Jas 5:16

preoccupied. Give it Scriptural readings, spiritual readings, Hagiography (saints' lives), meditations, psalmody, prayers. Allow these to enter into the depth. The stipulation is for the reading to be in depth, because if you read superficially it will not enter your mind and will not settle in you. Drift into the heavenly matters. Every mind has two layers: one mental layer is superficial and the other is profound. The important thing is for you to keep the spiritual in the profound layer. Sometimes when a person prays, the prayers are on the superficial level and the thoughts are in the depth, to the point that the psalm is finished and the person is unaware. Another one might drift from one psalm to another without realizing it, simply by coming across a sentence common to both psalms. Place the spiritualities in the depth. Deep reading and deep meditation are what protect you from drifting, but surface level readings have no effect.

Start your prayers with a spiritual preparation exercise. Do not switch immediately from the material to the spiritual, from preoccupation with work directly into prayer, use a spiritual reading, a song, a hymn, praise, self examination, meditation, or the saints' meditations and prayers in order to bring your mind out of the business of the day's work so that it engages in spiritual work. Do you know the story of the saint to whom the camel-driver came to take the baskets, and each time he entered the cell he forgot the request, until he tried to remind himself by repeating: "Weaving—camel; weaving—camel"?[89] This is because he gave the time and depth of his mind to prayer, not to the baskets or the camel-driver. To what do you give your depth? If you say you drift, that is ok, but what is the cause of your drifting, and how could you remedy yourself? Would someone who sits thinking all day long about the monastery, all its events, the guests, duties, and news, readily come to prayer? The mind will stray in all these issues, because they are still there, lingering.

Seek out the prevailing thoughts in your mind. What is on the surface, and what is in the depth?" Try to set up a substitution system where one thought replaces another, on the condition that the replacing thought is deeper. One

89 Saint John the Short (Ward, Sayings 1984), 92.

of the saints said, "Repentance is replacing one desire with another."[90] Instead of desiring the materials or the worldly, one desires God. Likewise, replace the worldly thoughts with spiritual thoughts. The person who prays continually is what they call the "working-monastic," not the one who is working in architecture or agriculture, but the one who is working in spiritual thoughts. This working monastic stores in the mind spiritual thoughts for the "years of famine"—the times when secular thoughts attack. Once a secular thought comes, the spiritual reserve comes out of the depth to overpower it.

Avoid the means which bring about secular thoughts that settle within you, or, avoid allowing them into your depth. Remember the psalm that says: "nor stands in the path of sinners"?[91] Do not allow your thoughts to stand in the path of sinners.

Filter out the warring persistent thought, the one that sleeps with you, awakes with you, and walks with you. You have to filter it out, because as long as it remains, you will drift with it; it is a persistent enemy. This is similar to a person with an abscess or a septic focus, which brings along a fever and a headache, no matter what painkillers you take there is no relief, you have to drain out this septic focus and then you will find relief from it, the headache, and the fever. Search out your septic focus. What thought persistently wars against you? Some issues might need internal and external filtering. For instance, a disagreement between you and one of the other monastics would need purification, otherwise you will continue to drift in it; either you filter it spiritually in your heart internally through humility and self-condemnation, or you filter it externally with the person you disagree with, or both. If a desire dominates you, you have to purge it internally within your heart, and externally by avoiding its causes, or else you will drift in it.

Warring thoughts might be residual thoughts in the subconscious from the past. Honestly, these thoughts need two things: time (until your subconscious is purified of them), and lack of use. As I remember, in the first year of

90 Cf. (Ramfos 2000), 233.
91 Ps 1:1

my monasticism, I dreamt of what was in my subconscious (a teacher in the Theological Seminary, an instructor in the Monastic Academy, a Sunday School servant); as a monk I dreamt of myself in my secular form because this form had remained with me for thirty years, but with time this image faded and my dreams consisted of the monastic image. Based on this I say that the objects in the subconscious need time until they fade away, on the condition that they are not used. With time they will fade away. Would the monastic name and image be imprinted onto the brain once you become a monk? This takes time until it is ingrained. As for your secular name and image, you have to endure not using them, and with time they will fade away.

Perhaps drifting is a war from the devil; the important thing is for you to fight the war. One might say, "A thought urges me. Although I reject it, it continues to press me." It is a war. Continue to fight it and never give up. Even those thoughts that are a war from the devil need mental and emotional concentration during prayer, and refraining from engaging the warring thoughts.

Depth in Prayer

For prayer to be without distraction it needs to be with understanding and depth; superficial prayers could be distracted, such as someone who races through the psalms without understanding or feelings. As St. Isaac said, "If you are fought with this issue say, 'I did not stand before God to count phrases.'"[92] I am standing to pray, not to count the number of psalms or lines. The more prayer is with understanding and depth, the further away it is from distraction. Therefore, often, the more a person memorizes the psalms, the faster the psalms are recited without understanding. One rushes through the psalms feeling nothing of prayer. It needs understanding and depth. Similar are those who memorize the psalmody and race through it, they do not benefit internally; neither their heart, nor their mind benefit, but it is simply about

---

92 (Miller 1984), 366.

keeping the rhythm of the hymn and words without benefit. The angels wonder, "Did they not pray today?" The monks answer, "We prayed the entire psalmody." To which the angels reply, "Nothing has reached us." Why did it not reach the angels in heaven? Because it was without understanding or depth. The more your prayer is with understanding, depth, reverence, spirit, faith, and feeling that every word has a meaning, the less likely you are to drift. If you take some of the psalms as an object of meditation, every word would have depth in your heart, and then when drifting thoughts come, they would be unable to overpower you. Why? Because each word would have depth in your heart. If a microbe comes to a very healthy person, what could the microbe do? Nothing. However, if one's health is weak and sickly, the microbe remains, saying, "This is my resting place forever; here I will dwell";[93] the thought finds an opportunity. If your prayers were deep and with understanding, it will prevent drifting! Bishop Abraam of Fayoom would sometimes spend two or three hours praying psalm fifty.[94]

I remember, one time when I was at the monastery, a spiritual monk from another monastery came to visit and stood to pray (he did not notice my presence. I remember this, as if it happened today, although approximately 43 years have passed since.): "Lord, give me many fountains of tears as you gave long ago to the sinful woman."[95] He stood drifting in prayer: "Lord give me many fountains of tears to cry over this … and this … and that." From the abundance of his requests he kept repeating that phrase and never finished. The phrase stuck to his mind and took on an emotional atmosphere with understanding, and he kept repeating it; meanwhile sometimes this phrase passes by us and goes without ever reaching our heart. We pray saying, "Let my supplication come before You."[96] How will it come before Him? It comes when it is with depth, understanding, purpose, reverence, love, and faith; all these qualities make the prayer link. See what it says, "Elijah was a man with a nature like ours, and he prayed earnestly

93 Ps 132:14
94 See (Malaty 1995).
95 From the Triparia of the Second Service of the Midnight Prayer.
96 Ps 119:170

that it would not rain."[97] Are they not all prayers? No, his prayer was serious, not simply words. Perhaps this reminds us of when the deacon stands (at the beginning of the Liturgy of St. Gregory) saying: "Stand with attention."[98] "Prayer" in Arabic means link, a link between you and God. What does this mean? It means there is connection. Similar to a high power electrical chandelier, if there is no link to the power outlet it is ineffective. When does it become effective? When there is a wire that connects it to the power outlet. Likewise, does your prayer have a connection?

One of the most beautiful prayers mentioned in the Bible is the prayer of Hannah the mother of Samuel. She prayed from her heart, her tears flowed, and she took a vow; she was praying with all her emotions. If you tell me that you drift in prayer, I will tell you that certainly not all your emotions are praying. If you were praying with all your emotions and all your understanding, then you would not drift. This is why St. Paul says, while combating the issue of speaking with tongues, "that I would rather speak five words with my understanding ... than ten thousand words in a tongue."[99] Pray with understanding. Try to mean every word you say in prayer with all your heart and all your mind, not just your tongue. What do we say in the psalmody? My heart and my tongue praise the Lord.[100] If I only pray with my tongue, it produces no results. Hence, prayer will be trivial to our lives, praying only if and when time permits, and thus our thoughts will wander in the present life, and give distraction an opportunity to take over our minds.

QUESTIONS AND ANSWERS

Q: You said it is better not to be preoccupied with work inside the monastery. Then, is it better not to work? Will the monastic's day therefore have a vacuum? The vacuum leads to sitting on the ledges.

---

97   Jas 5:17
98   (Aboseif 2000), 91.
99   Cf. 1 Cor 14:19
100 Kiahk melody.

A: I did not say you should not work, but I said you should not be worried over work. There is a great difference; you could work without mentally being preoccupied with the work. You work with your hands, but your mind is not occupied, or at least your senses, feelings, and thoughts are not occupied. We all have worked. You should use the free time in a spiritual way, but this does not exempt you from work. What did the fathers do regarding work? One works because work prevents the vacuum in which devils nest. One was not able to fill this whole vacuum, and so one worked and was preoccupied with the work. The more one grew in the work of prayer, the less one worked manually, until the work of prayer is complete, and then one does not work manually, being preoccupied with prayer. However, the person who neither works nor prays abandons the mind for the devils to work. I want your mind to be preoccupied with God, and if you find a vacuum, fill it in a spiritual way. If you are unable to fill it in a spiritual way and you find that the thoughts will trouble you, it is better for you to sit with people than to sit with the devil. It is better to sit with God than with people; but to sit with people is better than sitting with the devil. Therefore, retreat is not simply for a person to sit alone, but to sit with God; it is retreat from people, but unity with God.

Q: Technology has reached monasteries, and therefore now there are electronic equipment and objects that need deep mental concentration.

A: There are elements that technology offers that run automatically, not distracting one to think of them, while others need a person to think. Certainly it will not take all your time because the equipment is electronic.

Q: If a monk seeks the life of solitude but the monastic atmosphere does not promote this, would you advise him to go to another monastery with more suitable conditions?

A: No, I advise him to be under the direction of a spiritual father who would advise him as to whether he is fit for solitude or not, because there are people who think that they can enter the life of solitude, while their spiritual maturity is not ready for isolation. Like I said, the one who enters the solitary life is one who grows in the life of prayer, and the more one grows in the life of prayer, work decreases until one goes into the life of isolation. I'm sorry to say that we have seen people enter the life of isolation for one of the two following reasons (certainly there are people who entered the life of isolation out of love for God, and these are good examples): 1) to find respite from community work, or 2) to become a spiritual guide to others—"The solitary in the cave to whom people flock"—and in this case he does not live in isolation. One who wants to truly live the life of isolation, is one who occupies his mind with prayer and meditation, so that he is capable of doing the spiritual work.

Q: What is the difference between prayer at church and prayer in the cell? Does the church prayer suffice if one is busy with work?

A: Certainly not! In church the psalms are distributed, you might pray one psalm for two canonical hours; meanwhile in your cell you will pray them all. In church it is quicker, but in your cell it is with meditation. It is not right for the church prayers to make you forgo the cell prayers. In church we pray with one spirit in the fellowship of the spiritual life, and fellowship in prayer, but your personal prayer provides the opportunity for meditation, understanding, and praying your entire spiritual canon.

Q: I love solitary life, but the more I distance myself from services and mingling, the more I find it pursuing me. If the monastery's atmosphere is conducive to be around people, then how can I grow in solitary life in the monastery?

A: Again, I tell you to mature in prayer. Solitary life does not mean for you to sit alone; solitary life means you sit alone to pray. Try to mature in prayer, and if you are successful in prayer, the monastery will allow you to live the solitary life.

Q: Many times I become engaged in research regarding the canonical readings of the monastics, and spend much time in this. Would this be considered part of the canon?

A: There are beneficial monastic researches, in regards to the monastic or ascetic life, but when one becomes preoccupied with theological books, one tries to teach everyone what one has learned, regretting the loss if no one benefits from the researches you read in the spiritual books, and in the theological books. One might think, "If people do not benefit from what you learn, then what is the benefit?" So beware of being fought with the desire to teach others.

Glory be to God forever. Amen.

MONASTICISM: THE JOYFUL LIFE

November 28, 1992

In the Name of the Father, the Son, and the Holy Spirit,
One God. Amen.

The wise person sets balances between the many virtues in the monastic life. Take for example the virtue of mortification (putting to death the earthly physical senses), St. Paul instructs, "Put to death your members which are on the earth."[101] However, this virtue should not result in a person living a life of sadness, because St. Paul also says, "Rejoice in the Lord always. Again I will say, rejoice!"[102] and "As sorrowful, yet always rejoicing."[103]

"Rejoice in the Lord Always"

In self-mortification the spiritual person should feel joy, because mortification is the passive aspect in spirituality, and not the positive aspect. In mortification one rejoices because the spirit has conquered the body, the spiritual element has conquered the material, the two come together. Between himself and God, St. Arsenius shed more tears than most saints,[104] but before people he was cheerful.[105] If we have a sad countenance, people will either take a harsh impression of religiousness, or they will fear religiousness altogether. They will claim that you live in constant depression as a result of your relationship with God. The Bible says, "Rejoice in the Lord always"; you should appear joyful—rejoicing in

---

101 Cf. Col 3:5
102 Phil 4:4
103 2 Cor 6:10
104 Cf. (Ward, Sayings 1984), 18.
105 Cf. (Ramfos 2000), 95.

mortification—like one who overcomes the self and rejoices in the conquest. Why should we live in sadness? We have to rejoice that God released us from the present world's bonds. As I said today to the new nuns, "Rejoice that you were released from the present world's bonds, because many girls want to be nuns and are unable. Perhaps they are rejected by monasteries, their families or their community commitments hinder their path, their age blocks the way, or for any other reason." Those whom God preserves to continue on this way have to rejoice in God.

Rejoice in the Lord. Rejoice that you have time to pray, something secular persons do not have; rejoice that you have time to retreat with God, something secular persons do not have; rejoice that each one has her own private cell in which she spends her private time in a secluded calm atmosphere, which many people seek and could not find; rejoice that your monasticism as nuns is better than the monasticism of monks, because sometimes when a monk's monastic and spiritual life matures they commission him with responsibility (sometimes it is a war, and it becomes hard for him to leave his responsibility), but you are not concerned with worldly duties, this works to your advantage. In this point Orthodox monasticism is different than Catholic monasticism where their nuns are employed in schools, hospitals, and community service, meanwhile your church gives you the opportunity to live the life of retreat and tranquility. There are many things that call for the person to rejoice in the Lord.

This joy is for spiritual reasons, and is present even in prayer. Imagine, when David said, "I was glad when they said to me, 'Let us go into the house of the Lord,'"[106] what about the ones who live inside the house of the Lord! He says: "Blessed are those who dwell in Your house; they will still be praising You."[107] In the Psalms of David you will often find the expression "My heart rejoices," he is simply happy with God. The only sadness a person should feel is sadness over sins, but even this sadness is mixed with joy. How? In the "repentance psalm" (Psalm 51), where David condemns

106 Ps 122:1
107 Ps 84:4

himself before God for his sins, "Have mercy upon me, O God, according to Your lovingkindness,"[108] he also says, "Restore to me the joy of Your salvation";[109] the word joy is found even in the repentance psalm.

Rejoicing Even During Trials

You will experience joy in God's salvation very often; even amid trials God saves us. When the Israelites were very troubled before crossing the Red Sea, Moses the prophet told them, "Stand still, and see the salvation of the Lord ... The Lord will fight for you, and you shall hold your peace."[110] Therefore, a person can rejoice even amid trials: "My brethren, count it all joy when you fall into various trials,"[111] because in trials we feel how the hand of God intervenes, we feel the divine work, and we feel the salvation of the Lord: "Stand still, and see the salvation of the Lord.... The Lord will fight for you, and you shall hold your peace." Not only does He fight the external enemies, He also fights the internal enemies, a person's internal troubles. You might say, "God I can't fight my thoughts," and so, God fights against the thoughts for you; or, "God I can't fight my feelings," and so, God fights against the feelings for you. When Christ says, "In the world you will have tribulation; but be of good cheer, I have overcome the world,"[112] how does that benefit us? "No, just as I overcame the world, I continually overcome it *in* you, the worldly inclinations within you." The spiritual person feels that God has swung open the "door to delights" while you are still on earth (delighting in our Lord); secular people delight in the world, but the godly person delights in our Lord and continually takes pleasure in our Lord. This is what I want: for you to live continually happy and joyful.

Sometimes, when a person appears depressed, people start asking, "What ails you"; as a result, if everyone starts

108 Ps 51:1
109 Ps 51:12
110 Ex 14:13–14
111 Jas 1:2
112 Jn 16:33

questioning, you may be subjected to trials and temptations. How easy it is for people to start asking you about the reason for your depression. We should not repress ourselves, nor should we place ourselves on exhibit and in return become obligated to explain ourselves to people. Our lives have to be displayed in secret before God, even our sorrows have to be confidential before God.

The message of joy began the instant Christ came to earth: the angels chanted, "goodwill toward men,"[113] the angels told the shepherds, "I bring you good tidings of great joy which will be to all people,"[114] people rejoiced, all the angels chanted, and all who came in contact with Christ rejoiced, even the Samaritan woman's sorrow turned into joy when she met Christ. Christ said, "I will see you again and your heart will rejoice, and your joy no one will take from you."[115]

Love Leads to Joy, and Joy Leads to Peace

There is something nice in this thought of joy. When St. Paul spoke about the fruit of the Spirit he said: "The fruit of the Spirit is love, joy, peace."[116] This means that a person loves God, and once you love God you feel joy at finding this God and delighting in Him, and therefore you find that peace has filled your heart as a result of this joy. We find that love, joy, and peace are a triad to one spiritual work: you love God, you rejoice that you enjoyed God's love, and then you feel internal peace because you found God, found love, and found this joy.

Depression

In the *Apophthegmata Patrum* (sayings of the saintly fathers) we find that they were subjected to what are called the eight thoughts warring against the self. These eight thoughts are found in John Cassian's book *The Institutes*. This book consists

---

113 Lk 2:14
114 Lk 2:10
115 Jn 16:22
116 Gal 5:22

of 12 chapters; the first four chapters are concerned with monasticism in the early church (especially the Copts), while the other eight chapters focus on the eight thoughts warring against the self. St. Evagrius (along with many other saints) also spoke of the eight thoughts warring against the self. Among the eight thoughts is the war of depression.[117] We want every person who finds God to be happy and jubilant. You will find that the phrase "Alleluia" (praise the Lord) is found at the end of many psalms, as well as other phrases such as, "rejoice in the Lord," "exalt," and "rejoice."

Someone who had converted to the Blemmyes wrote a book attacking the Horologion (the Agpeya). Along his attack he said that anyone who reads the Horologion finds that it bathes in a pond of tears. My response to him on this point was that the expressions of joy are found in the psalms of the Horologion. It is true that the litanies have much self-contrition, but many of the psalms have expressions of joy, such as "praise the Lord" or "rejoice in the Lord"—many, many expressions! The monastic should be a person to whom this expression applies: "Oh, taste and see that the Lord is good."[118] The one who tastes God should be happy, joyful, and ecstatic in God. All worldly concerns are considered petty in comparison to this joy in God; it is enough for one to have found God.

Joy and Tears

The apostles passed through so many hardships, and even when they were beaten, stoned, and imprisoned, the Bible says that they went out "rejoicing that they were counted worthy to suffer shame for His name."[119] Many of the martyrs, while in prison before martyrdom, were singing praises of joy, because at least their uninterrupted encounter with our Lord was drawing near. It is true that they encounter God on earth, but the world takes away time; when they are martyred they will live with our Lord forever. Let each one ask how adhering

117 Cf. (Corinth 1979–95) Vol 1, 45–46; 87–88.
118 Ps 34:8
119 Acts 5:41

to God has brought joy to your heart internally. Search for the expressions of happiness, joy, and rejoicing in the psalms, especially in Psalm 119 and the psalms of the third, sixth, and ninth hours. You will find many amazing reasons for us to rejoice in the Lord.

Even when God finds us crying He says "[I] will wipe away every tear from their eyes."[120] Why? Because He cannot endure seeing us this way. He wants to call us to eternal bliss (to taste the Kingdom), even while we are still here on earth. He wants all people who see us to see that we are joyous in our Lord, saying, "How much we wish to live the life of those people, and rejoice like them in the Lord."

"Rejoice in the Lord always. Again I will say, rejoice!"[121] What does "always" mean? Think about it. It means that at no time can our joy be taken away from us. He says: "Your heart will rejoice, and your joy no one will take from you"[122]— no obstacles, neither internal nor external. You might ask, "Does this mean one should not weep over sins?" Weep (with joyful tears) but do not weep over your sins before people. Sometimes while you are weeping you will feel great grace in your heart even while you are still weeping, like St. Arsenius who lived happily, although he was well known for his tears. Life with God gives that kind of joy and pleasure. St. Paul says, "Therefore I take pleasure ... in distresses."[123] Often we tell people that whenever we found hardships on the way, this is when we know that this was our Lord's way, and we are comforted. He told us that His way is narrow and difficult,[124] so once I find a difficulty I say, "Yes, this is exactly the path of our Lord"; I rejoice to have found the path, and to have found a spiritual experience through this difficulty. Many people have amassed vast experiences through their hardships, and rejoiced over them.

Even for those who are currently disturbed (perhaps from a long-term hardship) there is reason to rejoice: "Rejoicing in hope."[125] They should have hope that their situation will improve, and rejoice in this hope. One should always say, "Even if things are turbulent our Lord will come, even if He comes in the last watch of the night," and therefore lives happily, rejoicing that God will come. Joy is not over receiving the promise, but in anticipation of receiving the promise. The one who received the promises is one who rejoices in what is seen (not in hope), but rejoicing in hope is for a future event.

Joy and Wars

We are not saddened by the devils who war against us, but rather we rejoice over the angels who fight for us. Gehazi was sad when he found the city surrounded by enemies, but Elisha was happy. When he found that Gehazi was sad he said, "Lord, I pray, open his eyes that he may see ... those who are with us are more than those who are with them."[126] When his eyes were opened he found the city was surrounded by the heavenly soldiers protecting them. A person has to live happily, and find delight in worship. In the great psalm (119) we find the phrases "my delight" ("Your law is my delight"), and the word "rejoice" ("I rejoice at Your word as one who finds great treasure")[127] often mentioned. We have God's words, do we rejoice in them? Do we rejoice in prayer, saying, "I will lift up my hands in Your name. My soul shall be satisfied as with marrow and fatness,"[128] and is our soul satisfied? "A good report makes the bones healthy"[129]—even the gospel is called good news (the literal meaning of the word "gospel") because it brings us good news.

Some wars bring sadness, as King David says in the third psalm: "Many are they who rise up against me. Many are they who say of me, 'There is no help for him in God.' [But will I believe this? Never!] But You, O Lord, are a shield for me, my glory and the One who lifts up my head. I cried to the

125 Rom 12:12
126 2 Kg 6:17, 16
127 Ps 119:162
128 Ps 63:4–5
129 Prov 15:30

Lord with my voice, and He heard me from His holy hill."[130] Sometimes one marvels at David. He prays, asks, feels that his prayer is heard even while he is still praying, and rejoices at the answer. In this same psalm where he began with, "Many are they who rise up against me," he continued, "but You, O Lord, are a shield for me, my glory and the One who lifts up my head." He rejoiced. At the beginning of the psalm he spoke of his hardship, and ended with joy. I want you to always be joyful. I want everyone who sees you to see the joy in your hearts: joy in your features, joy in your interactions, and joy in your whole life. This will cause people to rejoice with monasticism and say, "O that we could become nuns like those nuns who are always joyful!" They will exclaim: "They have, 'crucified the flesh with its passions and desires ... For Your sake we are killed all day long,'[131] endured spiritual exercises, offered prostration, fasted, and are distanced from their families, and yet they are this joyful!"

What type of person would be sad? One who leaves the world but sorrows over leaving the world! But the one who rejoices in leaving the world says, "Thank you God for rescuing me from this world. I'm happy this way. It is enough for me to set foot inside the monastery; it is enough for me that I made it in, others were unable to enter. It is enough for me that I've completed the testing period and had put on the monastic garb. This is an inexpressible joy." Some people claim that they rejoice when they cry. I fear if you rejoice in tears, and not in God. Sometimes one might apply such pressure and squint the eyes just to reach tears, even if by force, and once the tears come one rejoices—rejoicing over the tears not over God. One could rejoice in God and not necessarily have tears.

---

130 Ps 3:1–4
131 Gal 5:24; Rom 8:36

Types of Tears

There are tears of joy, tears of sadness, tears of suppression, tears of depression, and many other types of tears (I've written about them in the book on *Tears*). There are tears of joy; for example, when Jacob the patriarch saw Joseph, he rejoiced to see him and "fell on his neck and wept on his neck a good while."[132] What kind of weeping was that? Definitely these were the tears of joy. He could not have been sad; he was happy to see his son whom he had not seen in a long time. There are several examples of tears of joy, and they move the person. One should not have a depressed heart. The hardest thing is to have a depressed heart, which leads to depressed features, and from there a person becomes distressed. This is a war, an external war, and the person has to conquer it from the inside.

As Sorrowful, Yet Always Rejoicing

If the reason for the depression is my sins, then I have to abandon my sins, and the depression will leave me; I cannot keep them inside. I have to rejoice in God and tell him, "Look Lord, I know you will save me no matter what. I am confident in this. I am confident that our Lord will work. If not now, then later." The hardships are external, never internal, otherwise, why does he say, "The fruit of the Spirit is love, joy, peace."[133] What is your standpoint on this verse? The difficulty might be on the outside, but on the inside there is joy; this is why he said, "As sorrowful, yet always rejoicing."[134] People would ask, "Who are these people who are overburdened, and everything is upside down all around them? They are probably very distressed?" This is what people think, and yet we are, "always rejoicing." "Rejoice in the Lord always," hang onto the word "always." Our Lord Jesus Christ also said, "Your heart will rejoice, and your joy no one will

---

132 Gen 46:29
133 Gal 5:22
134 2 Cor 6:10

take from you";[135] therefore this joy is enduring and contains no sadness. One who enters a relationship with God enters the life of joy and walks along this path always.

Joy does not mean laxity; it means joy of heart without laxity. One is cautious in life, constraining the self until it walks uprightly, and yet rejoicing from the inside. I always tell people that the narrow gate is narrow at the beginning. It is triangular shaped: at the beginning you find difficulty, and the farther you go, it widens, until you reach its wide base of joy. The beginning is the period where "the flesh lusts against the Spirit, and the Spirit against the flesh,"[136] but at the end, the more the body surrenders to the spirit, and the more the spirit takes its ease, the more the person rejoices saying, "He also brought me out into a broad place."[137] He took me out of the stage of war between the body (matter) and spirit, and brought me into a broad place—God's love, in which a person lives happy.

The Difference Between Tears and Depression

Here I want to make a distinction between tears and depression. A person may have tears but not have a depressed heart. You find God and so you rejoice in Him. If those who have found God are depressed, what then will those who live in sin and are away from God do? They are oblivious to their condition; they need someone to sorrow over them. I always say that, out of the entire Bible, people only zoom in on this verse: "For by a sad countenance the heart is made better,"[138] and overlook all the verses about joy. I want to ask a question: "What if I begin my spiritual life with a sad countenance in order for the heart to be made better, and the heart is made better, will I continue to have a sad countenance?" If I continue to have a sad countenance then the heart still has not been made better! I needed the sad countenance to bring me to a better heart, therefore if the heart became better

135 Jn 16:22
136 Gal 5:17
137 Ps 18:19
138 Eccl 7:3

then I should rejoice. Will I remain with a depressed face perpetually?

Notice another point: this verse is in the book of Ecclesiastes, and this is considered the book of repentance for Solomon (as Psalm 51 was for his father David). This book is a proof of his repentance, a proof that he tried everything and found that "all is vanity" and "grasping for the wind."[139] After he explained how he had lived in worldly pleasures and delights—"Whatever my eyes desired I did not keep from them"[140]—he found that all this was vain, and found that it is "better to go to the house of mourning than to go to the house of feasting."[141] The book of Ecclesiastes represents his stage of repentance (the stage of tears), but a person cannot remain their entire life making the heart better with a sad countenance. That would mean that you have not yet found God. As long as your heart is not better then you have not yet found God. If you find God then you rejoice in His presence, you rejoice that indeed by a sad countenance the heart has been made better, and therefore you will thank God that the heart is better and you will "rejoice in the Lord always." Also note that he says "by a sad countenance," not by a depressed heart. This is the starting point; we should not make the starting points our goal.

"Blessed are those who mourn, for they shall be comforted,"[142] does not mean we should remain mournful our whole lives; we begin with mourning and end with comfort. If we remained mournful our entire lives then what is the meaning of, "Rejoice in the Lord always," and, "Your heart will rejoice, and your joy no one will take from you"? This is a starting point, not an end point. Also, "Your sorrow will be turned into joy"[143] is a good verse because it means that sorrow is a starting point, but does not remain as an ongoing condition; it turns into joy. Likewise in [the verse] "Blessed are those who mourn, for they shall be comforted," the mourning leads to comfort thereafter. We cannot say that our

139 Eccl 1:2; 2:11
140 Eccl 2:10
141 Eccl 7:2
142 Mt 5:4
143 Jn 16:20

whole life on earth should be tears and sadness—one would lose hope. Otherwise, what is the work of the Spirit of God in the heart of the person? What is the fruit of the Spirit in your heart if you remain continually in this condition? If you are resisting the Spirit you will feel sorrowful, but if the Spirit is working in you, He will lead you to various types of joy, to rejoice in the Lord. The expression "alleluia," "rejoice," "be joyful," "sing," and "praise the Lord a new song," these are all types of joy. He says, "Is anyone cheerful? Let him sing psalms,"[144] and singing is evidence of joy. Let us compile a list of the verses on joy; I will write them in an article, because I am writing a book on the Horologion.

Joy is Contagious

A person not only rejoices, but also makes people rejoice along. Look at Luke 15, the chapter of repentance, the one with the parables of the lost sheep, the lost son, and the lost coin; here you will find many expressions of joy. The one who lost his sheep, "When he has found it, he lays it on his shoulders, rejoicing ... there will be more joy in heaven over one sinner who repents than over ninety-nine just persons who need no repentance";[145] the woman who lost her coin, "When she has found it, she calls her friends and neighbors together, saying, 'Rejoice with me, for I have found the piece which I lost'";[146] and the father, when he saw his lost son said, "It was right that we should make merry and be glad, for your brother was dead and is alive again, and was lost and is found";[147] he made a feast in the house and killed the fatted calf. Therefore, repentance means joy. It is impossible for repentance not to bring about joy; joy has to accompany repentance, as David said, "The joy of your salvation."[148] Joy over repentance is joy on earth, joy in heaven, joy for the angels, and joy to our Lord Himself. How could our Lord rejoice over our repentance,

---

144 Jas 5:13
145 Lk 15:5, 7
146 Lk 15:9
147 Lk 15:32
148 Ps 51:12

while we live in sorrow? Perhaps we sorrow that we grieved God's heart, but after we reconcile with Him, there is no need for depression. You may weep over your sins, you may be moved, but as Solomon says, "To everything there is a season, a time for every purpose under heaven… a time to weep, and a time to laugh."[149] Being sad has its time, but this sadness must turn into joy. As for continuous sadness throughout the life, this is what would bring about depression.

Take for example a monk or a bishop who weeps during his ordination, these are not necessarily tears of depression; perhaps he is touched. One who is ordained a monk is happy to be ordained, so when he weeps he is not weeping that he became a monk, he is weeping over how God's hand had brought him to the point of fulfilling his desire, and is happy that God brought him to this point of finally being able to put on this angelic garb. Tears during an ordination might not be tears of depression, especially during a monk's ordination. As for a priest or bishop it might be a feeling of unworthiness of the great responsibility set before him, and perhaps it will be similar to what I experienced when I was ordained a bishop (that day was the most I ever wept); it was because I lost the life of solitude and seclusion that I had wanted to live. I lost one way, but God wanted another, "Your will be done"; again it was not an ongoing condition: this is a person who submitted to the will of our Lord and began to walk on the new path our Lord willed. Therefore, once the hand was laid upon me to become a bishop (before the ordination ceremony by a few days), the following verse always stood before me: "O Lord, I know the way of man is not in himself; it is not in man who walks to direct his own steps."[150] I did not know my way, I thought I had another path that I wanted to live, but our Lord chose a different path, what could I do. Likewise, St. Mary never thought she would be a mother, but our Lord chose for her a different path, to become a mother, and "Your will be done."[151] Tears during ordinations are not due to depression; the whole church is rejoicing. Perhaps one is touched, perhaps one feels the responsibility, or perhaps it is

---

149 Eccl 3:1, 4
150 Jer 10:23
151 Mt 26:42

a change of path. One might weep, while heaven rejoices, and his heart is jubilating from the inside. Is the one who weeps while praying the liturgy depressed? No. The term weeping is different from the term depressed. The term "depressed" means a person is pressed (fallen under pressure).

Finally, the liturgy ends with psalms of joy, cymbals and triangles, timbrels and chorus: "Our mouth is filled with gladness and our tongue with rejoicing."[152] Why? Because this great mystery was "given for us for salvation, remission of sins, and eternal life,"[153] and so, people rejoice.

Glory be to God forever. Amen.

---

152 (H and H 2007), 244. From the inaudible Prayer of Thanksgiving at the conclusion of the Liturgy. Cf. Ps 126:2.
153 Ibid., 234. From the Final confession.

MONASTIC ASCETICISM

In the Name of the Father, the Son, and the Holy Spirit,
One God. Amen.

Today, I would like to speak with you about an important issue in the monastic life: monastic asceticism. Monastic life is essentially a life of asceticism, renunciation, and exile (death to the world). For a monastic, asceticism and renunciation lead to what is called the life of detachment—detachment from everything. St. Anthony obeyed the commandment instructing to "sell all that you have and distribute to the poor,"[154] and we have likewise entered in on this principle. How can it be that the commandment says to sell all that you have, and we begin anew to attain possessions! For a monastic, possessiveness is a type of backsliding and an abandonment of the monastic vows: obedience, chastity, and voluntary poverty.

Asceticism and Poverty

How could a monastic live the life of poverty—that is, possessing nothing? There is yet an even higher level than the level of poverty: the level of privation. A person might be poor, barely making it, having just enough on which to survive, but when one is in privation, this person is in need of something, but does not find it. This is how our saintly fathers lived. *The Paradise of the Holy Fathers* spoke much of possessiveness and the love of possessions—how one gains possessions and desires acquisition. It has been said that St. Pijimi the anchorite did not have anything in his cell, not even a container. He ate of the grass of the earth and drank of the dew on the tree leaves.[155] This is similar to what was said of St. Moses the anchorite.[156] A monastic should observe

---

154 Lk 18:22
155 Cf. (El-Soriany 1993), 139–143.
156 Ibid., 52–59.

the number of containers and furnishings in the cell and ask, "Do I really live the life of poverty? Do I possess, or do I not possess?"

Some people had asked a legal question: "Who inherits from a monastic?" The answer was that the monastery inherits from a monastic. However, there is a question that precedes this one: "Does the monastic have anything to be inherited?" This is supposed to be a person who vowed poverty and possesses nothing, so how could this person own anything to be inherited?

Asceticism and Extravagance

If we mention the life of poverty and the life of privation, then what shall we say of those who live a life of extravagance? The life of extravagance does not in any way agree with the monastic life. Extravagance comes in degrees. Perhaps part of the subject of extravagance is the issue of excess. Does a monastic keep what is essential only, or also what is surplus? What one considers surplus, another might consider essential. If you deem them necessary, then your monasticism has reached a different level. The true monastic rarely ever regards anything as essential.

Asceticism and Electricity

Long ago, for example, there was no electricity in monasteries, so our cells had no electricity. I had a solitary cell, and until the time I became a bishop it did not have electricity. Even until I became patriarch, it did not have electricity. I was living in it until the beginning of 1977 (I did not have a cell at St. Bishoy's Monastery yet), and, although I was patriarch, my cell had no electricity. Now, they set up electricity everywhere, and when they fixed up my cell, they set it up there as well.

Should electricity be esteemed as an essential or as a surplus? We ask because it is good to examine all issues. You might tell me that electricity is essential in order for a monastic to keep vigil, read, and write. Long ago, having no electricity, when we were unable to remain awake on the lantern light, we would spend that time in prayer or meditation. These are more powerful than reading or writing. With electricity, the highest degree one pursues is reading. Thus, the merit of prayer was decreased and diminished, because prayer does not need electricity. It would be better if you turn off the lights, so that no objects distract your senses during prayer. Becoming preoccupied by the light, a person's intensity of prayer may be decreased, that is, if you are reading; otherwise, you could sit and gossip with friends and enter into offenses. This use of electricity could be a cause of problems for you: the cause of sleeplessness.

With electricity comes the recorder, perhaps a recorder with other options (I do not want to enter into the other options). Next we enter into the issue of extravagance. First, we drank from the fountain, now perhaps from the refrigerator, because now we have electricity. The fridge could be stuffed with other articles, and now, where has the life of asceticism gone? I do not want to add more than this. What I want to say is for us to never forget that the monastic life is a life of asceticism and renunciation. It is never a life of extravagance.

Asceticism in the Dwelling

Likewise, monasticism is never a life of extravagance in the dwelling place. Each one is looking for comfort in the dwelling place and increases the level of comfort little by little. What means of comfort did our fathers have, who lived "in dens and caves of the earth?"[157] One slept on the floor; one who was more extravagant slept on a straw mat; the one who was even more extravagant spread out a blanket on the straw mat. Now, I do not know how you sleep. I am reminding you of the vow we took on the day we became monastics, the day they prayed the prayer of the dead on us. It is not simply a ritual; we have died to the world and "all that is in the

---

157 Heb 11:38

world."[158] The monk who decorates the cell and the dwelling place, and seeks luxuries in his internal life, would turn his residence into an empire full of comfort and pleasure if he became a bishop.

Asceticism and Money

Does the life of poverty agree with salaries and funds? In our days, no monk took a salary. It was documented legally, but did not exist in reality. One person took charge of all expenditures, and none of us owned anything. I recall that in the entire time I was a monk in the monastery, no money ever touched my fingers until I became a bishop. If you have money in your pocket, how are you a monastic? What is the condition of the monastic who collects money from people? Also, what is the condition of the one who befriends seculars and accepts gifts from them? What is the condition of the one who asks gifts from the monastery guests, in roundabout covert ways that are nonetheless understood? For example, one might ask a guest, "What time is it? Forgive me, because I have no watch." The guest would say, "Yes, I will get you a watch." The monastic responds, "No. No. No," but in reality is saying, "Yes. Yes. Yes!" until the guest buys the watch. What links monastics with seculars and befriending them?

Asceticism and Residence

When a monastic who has vowed poverty and asceticism goes down to the world for a couple of days, where does this monastic stay in the city? Are the days spent in the city true monastic days? Are they days outside monasticism? Not only is it a departure from asceticism, but also other things. Does the one who lives in the world live a life of asceticism?

---

158 1 Jn 2:15

Asceticism and Dress

Regarding poverty and clothing, *The Paradise of the Holy Fathers* says, "The monk should wear a garment of such a kind that he could throw it out of his cell and no one would steal it from him for three days."[159] What is the condition of our garments now?

Asceticism and Expansion and Abundance

One builds a cell, then, has a thought of adding a wing, a second wing, a third wing, a second floor, and a garden. What is happening here? A monastic is above the level of needs, not feeling a need for anything. If someone asks you, "What would you like me to bring for you?" When you sit to think, you should find yourself not in need of anything. If you begin to feel that you need something, then you have begun to enter the world, since the world is what will bring things for you.

Asceticism and Health

Long ago, a monastic who fell sick would cry, "Oh, God!" and would be healed by this word. Now one who falls sick cries, "Oh, pharmacy! Oh, doctor!" I'm not saying you should not go, I am just stating the difference between now and then. Long ago, monastics were the ones healing the sick with their prayers, and also healing themselves by their prayers, or else enduring the sickness. I am not telling you to reach the point of not needing doctors; I just wanted to mention this point.

---

159 Abba Pambo (Ward, Sayings 1984), 197.

Asceticism and Consumption

Some monastics had remained two or three days without eating or drinking anything. Remember the monk who said that for thirty years, "from the time I began to be a solitary, the sun has never seen me eating."[160] Also remember the monastic who did not know when the Great Fast began because his whole life was one fast. This is a renowned story:

> They announced that the Great Fast had begun. A monk passed by an elder and told him, "Father, the fast has begun." The elder asked, "What fast my son?" The monk replied, "The Great Fast." The elder responded, "I tell you honestly, I have been here fifty-three years, and I do not know when this fast you speak of begins, or when it ends. All my days are one."[161]

Now we look forward to the Saturdays, the Sundays, and the Holy Fifty Days. What would happen if a monastic lives out this festive rite!

What is our discipline regarding food, drink, and asceticism? Certainly, you are better off than others in other places, but we are to seek out the way of perfection in our spiritual life. Oh, that each of us would take on a training exercise. Ask yourself: "What things can I forgo in my cell? What extra objects do I have? What objects can I leave off, utilizing what is less?"

Asceticism and Outer Appearance

When a monastic is seen dressed in shabby clothes and is barefoot, as a means of asceticism, this image is rejected, and we have to dress nice and wear socks in order not to fall into temptations. Extremes on either side are incorrect. I am not telling you to go to the other extreme and walk barefoot. At the same time, there is no need for extravagance in dress. The middle road is appropriate. There is a second option:

160 (Ward, Desert Fathers 2003), 23.
161 (Beni-Suef Publication Committee 1977), 345–346.

some meet guests dressed well, but inside the cell, anything goes. There is a third option: one who is unconcerned if seen by guests or not ("Does one live for the guests or for God?"). The middle ground is best: dress simple, neither in extravagance, nor in noticeable asceticism like the example of a barefooted person.

Asceticism and Possession

The monastic is not the one who owns nothing, but rather the one who is owned by nothing. One who is owned by nothing is the one who is able to not own anything. You own because objects own you. You cannot say, "I could gather many possessions, and nothing will possess me." If nothing possesses you, then why do you possess all these objects? Unless they owned you, you would not have gathered them around you. Let us not play on words, but stick to the spiritual way. Do you own, or are you owned? You possess what possesses a desire in your heart, and this desire owns a part of the heart; otherwise, you would have left it if it did not possess you.

Does this contradict poverty? What about the monastic who owns but is not possessed by what is possessed? If you truly are not possessive, then you should try to leave it; here it will become apparent if you are truly possessed or not. Sometimes a secular person would tell me, "I smoke, but cigarettes have no control over me." So, I respond, "Ok, then leave them and show me." If you possess and are not possessed by what you possess, then examine yourself; if you left this possession, will you be troubled or not, will you feel that you have lost something or not?

If we see the old cells and how they were built, and the underground lavras built with palm rushes or by any means, then look at the cells now, we could see if we are living a life of asceticism or not. If we see the way they ate long ago, then see how we eat now, we would see if we are living a life of asceticism or not. This is why I said that whoever wants to live in a cell as a solitary monastic needs to live above, on the rocks. There will be no electricity or water fountains. You could not vacillate between the two sides: solitude means isolation, it means asceticism, it means prayer, silence, stillness, and non-possessiveness. Solitude with extravagance cannot be found in any monastic book or any biographies of the Fathers. Each one of you needs to debate this issue with yourself internally. St. Macarius made a good comment: "Judge yourself before others judge you."[162]

Conclusion

We are only recalling these issues in order to know what is true monasticism. I want to tell you something: wishes and desires never end. If you begin to enter into desires, you do not know where it will lead you, how it will increase, how long you will prolong in it, how it will control you, or how you will switch from one desire to another, until you lose your monasticism as a result of your desires.

All glory and honor is due to our God forever. Amen.

---

162 Ibid., 35.

THE TRUE MONASTIC LIFE

In the Name of the Father, the Son, and the Holy Spirit,
One God. Amen.

An Upright Goal

I would like to speak to you about the true monastic life and how a monastic lives it. Primarily, a monastic must have a sound goal; either a sound goal in coming to monasticism, or correcting this goal after coming to monasticism. Ultimately one must settle on a sound goal. The sound goal in monasticism is for you to free yourself to sit with God and to remain steadfast in His love.

The original sound goal of monasticism is the life of stillness, of solitude, of prayer, and of repentance. Some people think that growth in the monastic life is simply progression toward solitude: "One progresses from being a community monastic, to a secluded monastic in the cell, progressing until one lives in seclusion—the cave monastic." In truth, this is not the only goal of monasticism. There are other goals within monasticism, goals for purity of heart. One person might live in seclusion without yet having reached purity of heart.

Excelling in Virtues

In the history of monasticism, we find fathers who excelled in the virtue of silence such as St. Arsenius;[163] fathers who excelled in the virtue of tears and repentance over their sins, also such as St. Arsenius[164] and St. Moses the Black;[165] ones

---

163 (Ward, Sayings 1984), 9.
164 Ibid., 18 {41}.
165 Ibid., 141 {3}, 142 {6}.

who excelled in the virtues of humility and endurance such as St. Anasimone The Fool;[166] others who excelled in the virtue of love and serving others such as St. Moses the Black;[167] and yet others who excelled in the virtue of unceasing prayer such as St. Macarius the Alexandrian[168] and many of the anchoritic fathers; and others who excelled in humility such as St. Theodore the disciple of St. Pachomius.[169] Each one took a virtue and struggled along its path as much as possible. It was said of St. Bishoy that when he gained a virtue and then it was discovered, he would concentrate his effort on another virtue so as to conceal his virtues from people.[170] Importantly, for all these people, monasticism was primarily the life of virtue, the life of internal purity of heart. A person becomes aware of his mistakes, and tries to correct each one of them until they are all overcome. For this reason, monasticism was labeled "the life of repentance."

Repentance

Living a life of repentance means that one begins on the path of repentance, pursues his own sins, and remedies them. If you walk in the life of repentance in the monastic life, you will never become upset if anyone rebukes you, but rather you will rejoice that someone exposed your mistakes to you, so that you may now abandon them. You would not be upset because you are walking in the life of repentance. Those who walked along this path in monasticism were also given the virtue of tears over their sins. In monasticism, there are tears that are inflamed by divine love, tears from a sensitive heart easily moved to flowing tears, and tears of repentance, as the fathers say, "Sit in your cell and weep for your sins."[171]

166 (Vivian, Witness to holiness : Abba Daniel of Scetis : translations of the Greek, Coptic, Ethiopic, Syriac, Armenian, Latin, Old Church Slavonic, and Arabic accounts 2008), 47–49, 275–276; (Budge, The Paradise of the Holy Fathers 2008), Vol I 145–147.

167 (Ward, Sayings 1984), 132 {22}.

168 (Behr 2004), 148–149.

169 (Budge 2008), Vol. II 51 {174}, Vol I 272–273.

170 (Beemen 1981), 29.

171 (Budge 2008) Vol II 45 {156}, 314 {618}, Vol I 228; (Ward, Desert Fathers 2003), 121 {16}, (Ward, Sayings 1984), 63 {1}, 126 {2}.

Who of us now sets a goal of sitting in our cell and weeping over our sins? Perhaps, one such monastic giant is St. Sisoes, who, even at the time of his soul's departure from his body was asking for another chance to repent.[172] St. Sisoes is the one who lived at one point in the eastern wilderness on the mountain of St. Anthony. Therefore, among the internal goals of monasticism are the life of repentance, purity of heart, and discovering weaknesses and diminishing them in order to rid oneself of them. Like I said, such a person is not upset by rebuke, but rejoices in it, and is given furthermore the virtue of tears.

Repentant People are Humble

Also, a repentant person is humble. Monastics often say: "This one is more righteous than me. This one is better than me. This one is more pure than me. This one is senior to me. This one is stronger than me,"[173] seeing all people as better than themselves because they are walking in the life of repentance, and that gives them humility. In the life of repentance, one does not become upset with people, as this is the result from a broken self inside. Being upset at others is always associated with pride inside one's heart. Pride inside the heart causes a person to rage over honor; when one is angered, one rages. The person who is repentant is a humble person, accepting all accusations as less than the truth, saying with St. Moses the Black, when he was expelled by Pope Theophilus at the time of his ordination as a priest, "They have acted rightly concerning you, for your skin is as black as ashes. You are not a man, so why should you be allowed to meet men?"[174] He rebuked himself, not being upset even at those who expelled him, although they were the ones who initially invited him.

---

172 (Budge 2008), Vol. II 200 {109}.
173 Cf. (A. H. Vlachos 1994), 35; (Beni-Suef Publication Committee 1977), 186.
174 Saint Moses, (Ward, Sayings 1984), 139 {4}.

Gaining the Life of Repentance from the Monastic Community

The goals of monasticism are not limited to solitude. Believe me, my brethren, solitude in monasticism without repentance has absolutely no value. Solitude does not bring one to the kingdom of God, but repentance does. If the two come together then it is good. Solitude is very nice, but it needs to coincide with repentance; without repentance, solitude is valueless. In monasticism, even if a person does not enter into solitude, instead of being sorry over this loss, one should say, "I will walk along the path of repentance. This is within my means amid the community." Community life aids repentance more than isolation does. How?

A brother went to an elder once and told him, "Father, I live in serenity, not many sins trouble me (he was living in solitude)." The elder replied, "This is because you live in solitude, and that is why no wars come to you, but go to the community, live among the monks, and there you will discover that you have control over nothing but your walking stick."[175] Why? He will submit himself to the troubles in the community, endure them, and discover if he truly is internally pure in heart or not. Sit and uncover your mistakes. The most important thing in monasticism is to root out our mistakes. Many monastics discover the mistakes of their fellow monks, but do not discover their own mistakes. One could sink into community unsettlement and discuss the mistakes of others with you, but may never understand his or her own mistakes. Perhaps gossiping about the mistakes of others helps one to, seemingly, dismiss personal mistakes. St. Moses the Black was not so. He said, "The sands are my sins which are running down behind me and I cannot see them, and I, even I, have come this day to judge shortcomings which are not mine."[176] He thought of his sins continually. One time, St. Bessarion was sitting in a court of monks judging a brother whom they expelled from the community. The saint rose up and

---

175 Cf. (Ward, Wisdom 1997), 39 {138}; (Beni-Suef Publication Committee 1977), 373.
176 (Budge 2008), Vol. II 138 {542}.

left, saying, "Since they expel sinners, then I also need to leave, because I am a sinner like him."[177] One who dwells on personal sins lives the life of repentance. The first thing we want in monasticism is to examine ourselves, know our weaknesses, train on ridding ourselves of them, and live the life of repentance. This is one important goal.

The Life of Humility

Monasticism also necessitates a life of humility. Among the virtues of monasticism is internal humility (which is feeling that you deserve nothing) and relative humility (which is assuming that all people are better than you). With this humility you will live as angels, not becoming haughty over others, not blaming others, not being angry with anyone, not boasting over anyone, not seeking authority or ranks, and not saddened if you do not attain them. You live a life of humility. Many monastics lived this life of humility. Some people lived in humility, even though they were distant from the monastic garb and the monastic title. Take, for example, St. Reweis, who was a great saint, living a life akin to monastics, but did not put on the monastic garb or given the monastic title. He was not associated with any monastery. He was a monk without the garb, title, image, cowl, girdle, or a monastic name—even his name, Reweis, is the name of his camel. His name was Freig or Tegi, but not Reweis.[178]

A True Monastic

Some people have lived the monastic life without being ordained as monks, refusing to be ordained. This has not only occurred during the days of the saints; this continues to occur, even nowadays. Bishop Theophilus told us about a brother who lived in "El-Sourian" monastery during his days. His name was Brother "Awadallah," as I remember, and

---

177 Cf. Ibid., Vol. II 131 {500}; (Ward, Sayings 1984), 42 {7}.
178 (Hanna, The Holy Fathers in the Diptych of the Holy Divine Liturgy 1994), 176–181.

he lived maybe forty or fifty years in the monastery without being ordained a monk. When they offered to ordain him a monk, he excused himself. He lived as a layman all his life and was a virtuous person. Monasticism is not the black robe we don, nor is it the monastic image, but it is the monastic life. You would say, "This one is truly a monastic!" Are there monastics who are not truly monastic? Yes, there are. Some take the monastic name, without taking on the monastic life. They live as monastics in the monastery, but virtues do not dwell in their hearts.

The true monastic is a humble, calm, meek person who easily interacts with all people. You find that, in dealing with some people, things turn awry from the start of the conversation. If you say a word, they respond, "What do you mean by that? No. Now, that is enough!" Meanwhile, some people are more easygoing. Even if ordered to do something they easily accept it. If rebuked, they let it pass. If overstepped in rank or order, they let it pass easily. If anyone says a hurtful word, they let it pass easily. Or if forgotten (overlooked in rations or in greetings, while all others are greeted), they let it all pass by easily. They are not easily disturbed. The one who is easily agitated will be troubled and will also trouble all the other monks.

Monasticism is a life of virtue. I wish that each one of us would ask himself, "What is the virtue that I have gained this whole time that I spent in monasticism?" Let no monk tell another monk: "I am senior to you. I have been in monasticism for eight years, and you have only been here two years." The issue is not how many years you have been in monasticism; rather, the issue is how many years you have been working to gain and excel in virtue in the monastery. What virtues have you gained in all this time? In what have you been cautious and attentive, walking with the fear of God before your eyes? "Theophilus of holy memory, the bishop of Alexandria, once went to the mount of Nitria, and a hermit of Nitria came to see him. The bishop said, 'What have you mastered in your lifetime, abba?' The hermit answered, 'To return blame to myself always.'"[179] This is one virtue he had been working on

---

179 (Ward, Desert Fathers 2003), 154 {19}.

for forty or fifty years, until he attained it. What virtue have you attained?

Virtues

Once, someone told me, after reading John Climacus' *The Ladder of Divine Ascent* (this book has thirty steps), "I have not yet become a monk. The entire life does not suffice to attain one of these thirty virtues. When will I finish them?" Set before you these thirty steps. How many steps have you attained? Who has walked on those beginning steps of exile and death to the world? Who has continued on these other steps of renunciation, tears, repentance, obedience, and meekness? There are many virtues. What virtues have you gained in your monastic life? Is monasticism simply achieved when a person isolates himself in the cell for a few days or one who sits in isolation for a while? What are your virtues?

The Goal

Some people think the virtues in monasticism are progressing from a monk, to a priest, to a hegumen, to an authority in the monastery, to a bishop's deputy, to a bishop, to an abbot of a monastery. These are the ranks set before them, the priestly orders. Others see administrative ranks, while still others see ranks of responsibility in one place to responsibility in some diocese to a candidate to something in particular. These are deviations from the goal. Many people deviate from the goal in monasticism, and adopt other goals that they make for themselves and fantasize about them, virtually living their dream, seeking to please their own selves because their selves have strayed from the goal.

When you left your house, your family, your job, your city, saying, "I have to pursue the monastic life," and God's love was inflamed in your heart, at that time you had in front of you an image akin to St. Anthony, St. Paul, the anchoritic fathers, or other saints. Where did this image and this goal both go?

Did other goals enter into your heart? Have you forgotten the first goal for which you left your house? Is it enough for you to obtain with the cowl, the girdle, the black robe, the different appearance, the look of a monk, people calling you "father", addressing you as "your reverence, absolve me and forgive me," and the reverence offered to you as a monastic? What exactly have you taken from monasticism? Some people were more humble, gentler, more prayerful, and more connected with God before monasticism. What is your goal? What monastic goal is set before you, and how much have you grown in it? Are there deviations in the goal? And, to what extent? Is the reason why you left the world the same or has it changed to other aspects?

Monasticism and Prayer

Monasticism should be a life of prayer. Prayer is growth. Coming to monasticism, you pray the seven prayers of the Horologion (Book of Hours [Agpeya]), saying, "This is good, I had not prayed all these prayers previously." Then you find, alongside these seven prayers, the praises in the Psalmody. This is not enough. You find prayers from the saints and prophets to add. This does not suffice, and you train on prayer while walking, while working, and while sitting with people. Finding this to still not be enough, you find delight in prolonging prayer, in keeping vigils at night in prayer, remembering the verse that says, "Behold, bless the Lord, all you servants of the Lord, who by night stand in the house of the Lord! Lift up your hands in the sanctuary, and bless the Lord."[180] You remember St. Arsenius, who would pray with the sun behind him at sunset, until it came before him.[181] Finding this to not be enough, you find unceasing prayer as the air continually inhaled and exhaled, but this is still not enough.

One asks, "What more?" This is all a measure of length in prayer, but there is yet the measure of depth. Where is the

180 Ps 134:1–2. All Biblical references are taken from the New King James Version unless otherwise specified.
181 (Ward, Sayings 1984), 14 {30}.

prayer with fervor, tears, understanding, humility, reverence, faith, love, and warmth? Where is the prayer in which a person feels that connection with God? One finds that the depth needs much time for the one virtue of prayer, and so one strives to grow in it. Each time a person asks you, "What have you done?" You respond, "I have a long way to go, I am just beginning. I am just starting on the road." Where is *this* prayer? What have you done in prayer? I have done nothing yet.

Stillness

One person enters monasticism saying, "Since monasticism is the life of stillness, I want to pursue the virtue of stillness," and begins to seek external stillness (stillness of the senses) then progresses to stillness of the mind, stillness of the heart, and stillness of internal emotions, becoming as the depth of the ocean which nothing dirties. No matter how the world is upturned around you, you remain extremely calm, living the life of stillness. Practice internal stillness, that is, stillness of the heart.

Another says, "How could I train on stillness when every time I come to calm down, this monk upsets me, and this other one irritates me? Is this stillness?" If a person is unsettled inside the heart, then all issues outside appear to be perturbing. If the inside is calm, then everything appears calm. Even if the world is turned upside down, you would be as if not there. This is an extremely, deeply calm person, undisturbed and unperturbed by anything. Your facial features are serene. Your senses are serene. Your thoughts are serene. Your emotions are serene. Nothing inside you is disturbed. Even your movements are serene.

One person might move and his motion is disturbing; feet are clumping, hands are swinging, the noise is loud, disturbing others. Even at work, one might be disturbing. On the other hand, for the person moving along growing in the life of stillness, everything is calm: calm expressions, calm features, calm speech, and a calm heart internally.

Self-Examination

I fear lest to us monasticism might be simply titles. If one asks you, "What is monasticism?" you reply, "As it is written in the books: monasticism is the life of unceasing prayer; monasticism is the life of stillness and calmness; monasticism is the life of repentance; monasticism is purity of heart; monasticism is a life of celibacy." But what have you tasted of all this? We need to examine ourselves from time to time. Self-examination is a great virtue. It is necessary on these occasions, when we remember monasticism, to audit ourselves akin to that saint who said: "What have we done that is as God wills, and what have we left undone of that which He does not will?"[182] Monitor yourself each day, as if it were the last day of your life. Examine yourself in order to strengthen yourself, to weep over your sins and be humbled so that when you see your weaknesses you will be gentle dealing with the weaknesses of others, and to be occupied with yourself and not go outside it and be occupied with others.

This is monasticism: a person who takes each monastic virtue and uses it as the weights of the balance for self-gauging. These are the virtues with which you should weigh yourself. Likewise, be honest with yourself. If a certain path will lead you astray then avoid it, even by a thousand miles. If a certain thing leads you astray from your goal, then wake up. This is the monastic spiritual watchfulness. For seculars, watchfulness is waking up from sins. For monastics it is also watchfulness over the self and searching the monastic virtues, seeing what you have, what you have lost, what you are missing, and what needs more effort, prayer, fasting, and clinging to God, and clinging to the horns of the altar[183] saying, "God help me. Help my weakness. I need special grace from You in order to make it." This is what we want.

---

182 Saint Nisterus, Ibid., 155 {5}.
183 Cf. Ps 118:27

To Dwell in the House of the Lord All the Days of My Life

I thank you for sitting with me on this day. I am grateful for your love, but what is important is that we sit in order to remember our monasticism, remember how our life is moving internally. We are required to give an account to God for the spiritual abilities given to us. Some people wish they could stay in the monastery even for one night, and they say, "Thank You God for allowing me to stay in the monastery." If one stays a week, this is considered unmerited grace from God. What are you doing, you who are spending your whole lifetime in the monastery? What have you done with this talent,[184] the talent of living in the places of the saints? This talent of living in the house of the Lord all the days of your life, what David longed for and could not attain, saying, "One thing I have desired of the Lord, that will I seek: that I may dwell in the house of the Lord all the days of my life."[185] Here you are living in the house of the Lord all the days of your life, you fulfilled David's longing, and what have you done with it? When David remembers this he says, "Blessed are those who dwell in Your house; they will still be praising You."[186] You are of those who dwell in His house; do you praise Him forever? He also says, "Behold, bless the Lord, all you servants of the Lord, who by night stand in the house of the Lord! Lift up your hands in the sanctuary, and bless the Lord."[187] You live this verse exactly. Are you among His servants? Living in the house of God is a talent, for which you will give an account. See, have you traded with it and gained or not?

Some people envy you because you live in the house of God, because you are next to the church (the church is in your house), over the daily liturgies, and over the Midnight Praises. In the world, some people are as if under surveillance if they want to pray; they are embarrassed of some people, and they will be mocked if they stand up to pray. If one is exposed, it turns into an issue. You are given all those

---

184 Mt 25:14–15
185 Ps 27:4
186 Ps 84:4
187 Ps 134:1–2

opportunities. Some people envy you because each one of you has a separate room which no one enters, and you can close the door and sit alone with your Father in secret.[188] This is not available in other places. People envy you over this still, calm environment. Some people wish to live one of your days, and here you are living in the house of God, in this calm environment, in separate cells, next to the church, daily liturgies, the Midnight Praises, in a spiritual atmosphere, in a unified community with the one goal of loving God and being set apart for Him. What have you done with this talent? It is not only the seculars who envy you for this. It is even the bishops themselves who envy you for living in an environment they are unable to live in. What have you done with this talent? We need to ask ourselves.

You could find a secular person who might say, "Oh, if only they would give me a month to spend in the monastery, I would come out of it a saint." God gave you months and years, and what have you done with them? These are talents offered to us from God, in order to work with them. Say, "Thank you God for giving me this place, please give me the ability to work with it." One monk might find that a whole day had passed by without doing one spiritual task. Once a day passes without a spiritual task, realizing it, the alert monk would say, "I will make tomorrow worth two days." The slack monastic passes one day doing nothing, and another day, a third day, a week, a month, oblivious like a person in an undercurrent, not knowing where he is. The days pass by all the same, and his nature remains the same, and the secular nature before monasticism returns, and then you come to ask, "What have I taken from monasticism?" Perhaps visitors could disturb this personality type because they expose it. If one becomes a monk, relatives say, "I will find an earthly angel and a heavenly human," and come to visit but finds neither an earthly angel nor a heavenly human, and he did not change at all. It is the same conversation, the same style, the same method. They leave saddened proclaiming, "Nothing has changed!"

What then have you done to be one of the heavenly angels? Monasticism is among the angelic orders. I hope that

---

188 Mt 6:6

we would wake up and think about our lives, and try to work with the talent given to us. Work with the stillness given to you. Work with this life that brings all spiritual growth within our reach. If you say, "I am preoccupied in the monastery and am unable to live the life of unceasing prayer," I will tell you, "Okay, if not unceasing prayer, live the life of complete love, live the life of endurance, train on forgiving others, train on taking the sins of others and applying them to yourself, train on the gentle good tongue and good interactions, train on obeying everyone and serving everyone." There are many things you could do. Among the reasons of ungratefulness is that many times we think of the things that we lack, and do not think of the things made available to us. However, there is much that you are able to do. Therefore, let each one of us, after we leave, sit with our conscience even if for a little while saying, "I want to advance, even if one step. I want to see my flaws and fix them. I want to stop defending myself and stop justifying myself. I want to stop boasting over my intelligence, my ability, my talents, what I can do that others cannot, of the great feats I accomplish in the monastery those for which the monastery should thank me; I need to look inside myself and examine my mistakes in order to overcome them. I need to make my meeting with my father confessor a session of honest self-condemnation, not self-justification."

Sometimes, the father confessor sits before the confessor and is troubled inside himself wondering, "Should I speak or not?" When the father confessor has many children, twenty or thirty or forty, and each one admits personal sins and friction with others, the father confessor will know if this monk upset others in some situations. He knows the incidents in details, but the one sitting to confess may not bring up any of these issues. He asks, "Anything else?" The monastic responds, "Nothing else." What will he say; will he expose the confessions of others? He could not and at the same time, he is unable to believe that there is nothing else. He prompts you to think, but the confessor insists that there is nothing. What can the father confessor do now? This one is either lying, oblivious, or the spiritual values have deteriorated to the point that he cannot distinguish right from wrong. Such people need to return to the original values set in the lives of the saintly fathers, the fathers of monasticism, the teachings of the recognized first fathers of monasticism, such as the teachings of St. Anthony the Great, the Spiritual Elder, Abba Isaiah the Solitary, St. Barsanuphius, St. John of Lycopolis, and St. Philoxinus; the fathers whose words are like accurate scales, like spiritual mirrors; you look into them and see yourself. This is what we need. We need to take these scales and weigh ourselves on them.

We need to not only think of our mistakes, but also think of our growth: are we growing, or have we reached a certain point and then stopped? Some people's growth gets paralyzed; they reach a point and do not move any further. They might move backwards, but never forward, caught in a standstill position. Where is your growth? Where is your growth in monastic virtue, in prayer, in stillness, in loving God, in humility? Do you simply stand each day, raise your hands and say, "When the morning hour approaches, O' Christ our God the True Light, let the senses and the thoughts of the light shine upon us."[189] Do you simply say it? Do you feel that there is love between you and God? Do you feel that you have developed a relationship with God in monasticism? Do you feel that you have encountered God face to face in monasticism? Do you feel that God is in your heart, and that you are in His heart? Do you feel the emotions of love that ignited people who lived in the wilderness and crevasses without boredom because they delighted in God who dwelt within them? What has happened to you? Let us return to ourselves. As St. Isaac says, "If you fall astray along the road, sit with yourself,"[190] and remind Mary of her adultery and Israel of his defeat, remind yourself of your weaknesses, rebuke yourself greatly. As St. Macarius the Great advised, "Judge yourself before others judge you."[191] Also, "If we judge ourselves, the Judge will accept us."[192] "If we remember our sins, God forgets them; if we forget them, He remembers them. This is what

189 (Agpia: The prayer book of the seven canonical hours 1997), 23. This is taken from the Litanies of the First Hour.
190 Cf. (Miller 1984), 41, 462.
191 (Beni-Suef Publication Committee 1977), 35.
192 Ibid., 138.

we want to remember on this night."[193]

There are many books and monastic sayings, and we all have them. We could read them to see how we are doing, and how we should be traveling. Each one of you needs to wake up and begin thinking of your salvation. What other goal do we have in monasticism but to save our souls? We have no other goal. If we are traveling on a road that is contradictory to the path of our salvation, then we need to change and correct ourselves lest we find many laity who have preceded us to the Kingdom of God while we were oblivious. We find lay people who might love God more than we do, and who are, perhaps, more pure in heart than we. At least they might be more humble than us, while we consider ourselves fathers who have authority over others. They are small, and consider themselves to be small, and much less than us, no matter how high of a position they hold. I do not want to talk to you much more than this, because you know all this, but as the Holy Bible says, "Comfort one another with these words."[194] In order to reach the kingdom of heaven, we need to always ask God, in all our spiritual efforts, to give us the strength to take us there. At all times, pour yourself out before God saying, "O Lord, You who led St. Anthony, who lived alone in the mountain without a guide and without a predecessor (on the way) to show him the roadway when he had no spiritual father, and gave him Your wisdom, also give me this wisdom, a free gift from You. Oh Lord, who led St. Paul the Anchorite, living alone without anyone to support him along the roadway, please support me as You supported him. You who led Pelagia, Mary of Egypt, Augustine, and Moses the Black in the life of repentance, lead me as You led them." Always cling onto God, remain with Him always and say, "I will not let You go unless You bless me!"[195]

With time, if you find that you have walked on the right road and corrected your path, do not allow your heart to be exalted. Remember the very high ranks that the saints reached and ask yourself, "Where am I from those?" Can you poise your mind as St. Macarius the Alexandrian, or pray unceasingly

193 Cf. (Ward, Desert Fathers 2003), 85 {6}
194 1 Thess 4:18
195 Gen 32:26

like him? Have you reached the depth or fervor in which the saints lived? I have a long way to go. May the Lord who gave to all those, give us also that we may delight in Him and glorify His Name.

His is the glory from now and forever. Amen.

THE UPRIGHT GOAL

In the Name of the Father, the Son, and the Holy Spirit,
One God. Amen.

Regarding monastic life and keeping stillness, St. Isaac said
that there are three items that are necessary for a person
in order to dwell in stillness: the upright goal, fulfilling the
canons, and maintaining stillness.[196] He says that every person
is in great need of these three items.

First, Define Your Goal

The upright goal in monasticism is very important. Why did
you leave the world and come to monasticism? The answer to
this question determines your path inside monasticism. There
must be a goal, and it must be upright. Certainly, the one and
only goal is to love God. For the sake of the love of God, a
person leaves the world; if a person has any other goal then
it is to no avail. We say in the Divine Liturgy, "They dwelt
in the mountains and deserts and holes of the earth because
of their great love for Christ the King."[197] A person, out
of love for God, left the world in order to be dedicated for
God. If this is the goal, then the means must meet that goal.
As I see it, a novice approaching the monastery sets sight
on one of the following three means: growth in the life of
solitude, stillness, and calmness; the monastic life of service,
either inside or outside the monastery; or purity of heart via
the life of repentance, and gaining virtues, such as humility,
meekness, endurance, calmness, obedience, etc.

---

196 (Miller 1984), 189–196.
197 (H and H 2007), 431. This is taken from the fraction for the Holy Fast of the Forty
Days to the Father.

Next, Determine Your Means

If you seek to build yourself through monasticism, then the result will be that you will lose yourself and lose the monastery as well. You will turn into a self-loving person, and you will not be able to deal with the other members of the monastic community. Based on these three means (isolation, service, or purity of heart), your life in the monastery will be determined.

If, for example, you seek purity of heart and gaining virtues, then you will not care if you live in solitude or not. You will care about having a pure heart. You will care about interacting with people in order to discover your mistakes, remedy them, and train on abandoning them. You will concentrate on being blessed by everyone. This occurs through obedience to all, submission to all, considering all people to be better than yourself, and winning each person's love, as St. Anthony said, "Let everyone bless you."[198] Thus, you will not enter into the problems specific to solitude, nor will you seek isolation or try to pressure the monastery into allowing it. Your goal will be purity of heart.

If you tell me your goal is worship and unceasing prayer, then these will be your means to achieve the goal of loving God. The one who enters this arena will say, "I need solitude," because you will not be able to do this amongst people. In truth, you are unable to be devoted to worship until you have passed through purity of heart. Purity of heart comes first, and worship comes second. If you try to be devoted to worship without purity of heart, your worship will be unacceptable, and you might grow skeptical [lose your peace of heart]. For example, you may want to be isolated and set apart for prayer. Someone passes by you, and you react by arguing, shouting, and becoming upset; then you will become unsettled internally. But if you are calm on the inside, have gained meekness and humility, and then enter the life of prayer, and someone comes knocking at the door of your cell, you will then be able to resolve the issue with meekness

---

198 (Bishop Mettaous 2005), 78; cf. (Budge 2008) II, 8 {14}; (Beni-Suef Publication Committee 1977), 198.

and calmness.

Some people assume that they are not monastic unless they grow in the virtues that have to do with the body. It is not considered a true virtue if it is simply physical; virtues need to be spiritual. I am speaking of the virtues related to the body, such as fasting. One says, "I have to enter monasticism and grow in fasting, until I reach a certain level of asceticism and a certain degree of abstinence. Perhaps I will fast days at a time, perhaps abstain from certain types of food that I will not eat for the rest of my life, not even on feasts. They set their sight on the sayings: "The sun has never seen me eating,"[199] and, "If it is meat, we do not eat it,"[200] and, thus, one becomes focused on these things. Another might assume that monasticism is asceticism of the body in dress, in dwelling, in poverty, and in the apparent virtues, but forget the internal work inside the heart and purity of heart. You might only seek a certain number of prostrations, a certain level of fasting, or a certain level of seclusion, but not give care to the state of the heart. You would not be concerned about whether or not your heart is humble, meek, tolerant, pure, or loving towards people; your whole concern would be prostrations, fasting, seclusion, and silence—the outwardly virtues. Because of this, you might lose the love of people, criticize others who do not fast like you, ask about the prostrations of others in order to compare yourself to them, or condemn those who do not go into seclusion like you—and you might find difficulty in this life.

In truth, if you want to follow an upright goal that is consistent with God's love, you need to first gain the virtues of living in the community, purity of heart, the life of repentance, the life of humility, the life of meekness, the life of endurance, the life of stillness, getting the blessings of all and winning the love of all, and placing yourself below everyone else. Thereafter, little by little withdraw, with guidance, until you fulfill the life of worship, the life of prayer, and the life of solitude as God allows for you.

---

199 (Ward, Sayings 1984), 114 {4}.
200 Ibid., 81 {3}.

Also Take Spiritual Food

The frame you set for yourself determines all of your other actions. An example of this is knowledge. With what type of knowledge are you concerned? One person places emphasis on the Holy Bible and meditating on it, while another places emphasis on spiritual books, and yet another places emphasis on ascetic books that search into the monastic path and behavior, while another likes to read theological, research, or doctrinal books. One person differs from another.

If you set isolation before your eyes as your goal, then you may say, "I want to read St. Isaac. I want to read St. John of Lycopolis. I want to read the Spiritual Elder (John Saba)." You might begin with these, and you might also read the Philokalia. If you set service as your goal, then you might read about theology or doctrine, or the differences between the sects, religious knowledge, canons, dogma, theology, language, etc. If your goal is purity of heart, you will read spiritual books specific to purity of heart. You will try to apply what you have read more than trying to read more; you will focus on spiritual practices more than spiritual readings.

Be Deeply Rooted in Your Path

Truly, you need to have a clear goal set before you, and your means need to be clear before you. You need to know that each day, you are taking one step towards the goal, and taking a step forward on this goal. Otherwise, if you do not have a clear goal, or clear means by which you attain your goal, you will drift in monasticism aimlessly, without restraint, without self-observation, perhaps not knowing where you are, whether you have moved forward or backward, not knowing what you are doing. You might end up asking yourself, "Why did I become a monk? What benefit did I take of monasticism?" Perhaps you might fall into skepticisms and misgivings, or perhaps you might forget yourself. Each one of you must set the goal clearly before your eyes. This is why St. Isaac said that there are three items necessary for a person who dwells on this path: the upright goal, fulfilling the canons, and maintaining stillness.[201]

If you find that your goal is not clear or upright, try to remedy this. Sit with yourself and ask yourself, "Why did I leave the world and come here?" If we would only ask ourselves, "What is monasticism? Why did I come to it? Am I walking in it or not?" Also, ask yourself: "Am I progressing on this monastic path? Am I at a standstill? Or am I moving backward?" Of course, in humility, you will answer, "I am nothing," but by examining yourself you will see clearly whether or not you are walking correctly and you will attribute it to divine grace, so as not to be struck by vainglory. Also, if you are walking correctly, compare yourself with the role models in monasticism saying, "It is true that I am walking forward, but I still have a long way to go and I haven't even started yet." The important thing is for you to know where you are going, like the monk who used to say, "Where are we now?"[202] Where are we going? What are we doing? What have we fulfilled of the monastic life? Take it one step at a time.

Above All, Have Purity of Heart

Whatever means a monastic pursues (solitude, service, or worship), one needs purity of heart to be able to do any of these. Therefore, I will give you advice in the beginning: each one of you needs to set purity of heart as his goal, considering it the first step on the monastic path. Without purity of heart, worship is unacceptable. There are unacceptable prayers, as the Holy Bible says, "The prayer of the wicked is an abomination to the Lord."[203] The Lord did not accept the prayer of the Pharisee, neither the prayers of those to whom He said, "When you spread out your hands, I will hide My eyes from you; even though you make many prayers, I will not hear."[204] Yes, there are unacceptable prayers. For your prayers to be acceptable, they need to come from a pure heart. Likewise there are also

---

201 (Miller 1984), 189–196.
202 (Beni-Suef Publication Committee 1977), 396–397.
203 Cf. Prov 15:8.
204 Is 1:15

unacceptable fasts. As the Lord said, "Would you call this a fast, and an acceptable day to the Lord?"[205] Not all fasts are accepted. Worship must come from a pure heart. Likewise, if purity of heart does not precede the life of solitude, it turns from solitude into introversion, from a means of worship to the goal of fleeing from people, or intolerance of people, or as one of the fathers put it, "Such a person spends a hundred years in his cell, and does not even learn how one should sit."[206] Therefore, we need to place purity of heart as the primary goal before us. Purity of heart requires you to search yourself, know your mistakes, and work on them.

It is painful, rather sad, to find problems within the monastic life between monastics. Why is it sad? Conflicts occur in the world because laymen differ in their goals, means, religions, dogmas, principles, values, and role models. Also, large populations are more prone to conflict. In monasticism, there are a small number of individuals who have all left the world for one goal, all living in one house, eating at one table, praying in one church; they are a small group of brethren coming out for the sake of God and His love. Not only that, but this is a detached ascetic group in unison and faith in all the virtues and values, and are dead to the world. If this small, unison, religious, worshipping, ascetic group cannot collaborate, then this is a very dangerous issue, and applying our Christians principles would be difficult. If saints are unable to tolerate each other, then how much more could lay people? "If therefore the light that is in you is darkness, how great is that darkness!"[207] How could a small group not agree with each other? How could a small group have amongst them competition, collisions, conflicts, upsets, conflicting desires, condemnation of each other, and factions? This is hard. All this is caused by not placing purity of heart as the primary goal in life.

Perhaps one might object, "But, I have given purity of heart primacy in my life." I would respond, "Perhaps what troubles you then is internal pride." You do not confess that you have sinned, and therefore, you do not discover your

205 Is 58:5
206 (Hausherr 1990), 72.
207 Mt 6:23

mistakes, in order to remedy them. For you to reach purity of heart, you need to remedy your faults. In order to remedy your errors, you need to discover them and confess that you were wrong. If your pride prevents you from saying that you are wrong, and prevents you from discovering your mistakes, and you are continually justifying yourself and giving yourself an excuse for every error, then it is impossible for you to reach purity of heart. Purity of heart requires you to sit with yourself, be honest with yourself, judge yourself, condemn yourself, change yourself, rebuke yourself, and in all things return the blame onto yourself.[208] This is the requirement for one who wants to reach purity of heart.

Do Not Justify Yourself

Believe me, one of the hardest things in monastic life is finding monastics who are soft on themselves and want others to spoil them. If you are very sensitive about your personal pride, wanting others to honor you and give you special treatment, then you will have many requests that will come out as commands. Then you will be easily upset if your request is not answered, and you will become doubtful, grievous, ugly, whiny, and bitter toward everyone, and the issue will grow worse. All this could occur over a small unfulfilled request: "How could I ask, and they do not fulfill? Why do they treat me this way?" In all this, one forgets humility, meekness, endurance, and death to the world, but only wants self-comfort and wants to be pampered by others. Thus, the person who does not justify, but rather is strict with himself, wanting to overcome the desires of the self, needs to be honest: "I have this fault, and I need to change it to reach purity of heart. If we correct this, we can tackle another mistake, remedy it, and reach purity of heart, etc.," until one is fully purified, and becomes a monastic as should be.

I believe that each person who loses peace within monasticism loses it for non-monastic reasons. There are no monastic reasons for losing peace. Furthermore, a monastic

---

208 Abba Amoun (Budge, The Paradise of the Holy Fathers 2008), Vol II, 124 {461}.

is an angel; is there an angel who loses his peace? Is there an angel who gets upset? Unbelievable! If one of you gets upset, then you lose your image as an angel.

Glory be to God forever. Amen.

THE VIRTUE OF DETACHMENT

In the Name of the Father, the Son, and the Holy Spirit,
One God. Amen.

By God's grace, today we would like to speak about a virtue needed by all people, but especially by monastics: it is the virtue of "detachment." What does detachment mean? It means that a person possesses absolutely nothing. How can you live without owning anything? At least, in your heart, you are prepared to own no objects, no money, and no furnishings; you might sometimes find a monastic who has many items, perhaps tens of different things inside the cell. One comes to ask, "Where then is the virtue of detachment?"

Indifference to Increase or Decrease in Possessions

The virtue of detachment is defined by readiness to get rid of your possessions and not be saddened, and don't even think to increase them, and also not to be disappointed if they do not increase. Coming to the monastery, a person is prepared to not even have a dwelling place. But, when he gets a cell, he then begins to want a cell with a window facing North or South, well ventilated, on a higher floor or on a lower floor. Now he starts to involve his personal taste. Here we begin to ask: where has the virtue of detachment gone? If it is possible to have two or three cells, why not? Where is detachment! Detachment became something we vowed to long ago and forgot.

The person who possesses the virtue of detachment not only possesses nothing, but also does not long to possess anything: "Do not love the world or the things which are in the world."[209] To the one who longs to possess, the Lord

---

209 1 Jn 2:15

is not sufficient; aside from the Lord, one longs to possess other objects. Also, if one possesses other items, where then is the virtue of voluntary poverty?

Sometimes, a monk is upset for not receiving rations, not receiving equal rations, or not receiving a certain quality of the rations. A monk who has become detached to the world does not seek quality. Rather, one seeks the quality of the virtues. Fussing over the quality of the items, including whether the clothes are of good or bad material; whether expensive or inexpensive; whether the furnishings are good or not so good; wanting the carpenter to create an item specialized to their taste; wanting a fan because the air is not pleasant enough; being bothered by the tile, desires carpeting, a heater, and many other furnishings—this is a never-ending issue. When you ask where detachment went, you find that the person has been detached from detachment.

Indifference to Suffering Loss

Let me tell you another characteristic of the detached person. If a detached person has something, it is as if they do not have it; if it is lost, one is not troubled or saddened. If you lose a pen made of ebony, you would not become upset. If a watch breaks, it is okay. If you lose an object, you will not become distressed. If something is taken away from you, you will not be disturbed. If someone asks for an item, you will not be troubled. If you are wronged, you will not be offended. Why would a person who has died to all things be displeased over something that increases or decreases? If you are upset over a specific item, then you have not died in respect to that one specific item. There is a long section in the *The Paradise of the Holy Fathers* on this issue of possessiveness; please read it.

The Detached Is a Giver, Not a Collector

The person who attains the virtue of detachment gives more than receives, because in giving, one is released from the burden of the items one has, whereas the one who takes adds items to items. The major problem is when a person possesses items that he does not use, only to set them aside. "For what do you use them?" "It does not matter; it is something keeping me company in the cell." I do not want to be harsh on anyone, but I need to tell you that you will give an account of every item in your cell that you do not use and is only set aside. There might be a person who is in need of it.

What is even worse than having unused items in your cell, is allowing them to stay in your cell until they are ruined and neither you nor anyone else was able to use them. For example, consider a person who holds on to a few extra clothes beyond need, until they are eaten by moth and neither he nor anyone else has benefitted from them. Another person might have unused clothes or paper, etc., that remain unused until a mouse chews on them, and neither this person nor anyone else has benefitted from them. There is a monk who takes only what he needs, while another takes everything distributed, regardless of need. It just sits there. Where, then, did the vow of poverty go? Is this a glance backward? The Bible says, "No one, having put his hand to the plow, and looking back, is fit for the kingdom of God."[210] Has the person sold the world on the day of his ordination as a monk, only to begin to build a new world after monasticism? You discarded possessiveness when coming to the monastery but began anew to gather possessions? Each individual needs to ponder this issue personally.

Another important issue: how can a person own anything after dying to the world? Officially, all that is in your cell belongs to the monastery, and you are simply borrowing it—an ongoing loan—you do not own anything. Alas, let us not blame the many possessions, but ask if your heart is prepared to abandon them or not.

---

210 Lk 9:62

Excesses and Necessities

Here we come to the question: "Should I forgo items in excess of my need?" This question is put to shame by the story of the widow who gave from her needs.[211] If you only give up items that you do not need, then you are not giving from your needs; if you are in need of something and you give it despite that, then this is true detachment. The person who is "detached," in the deepest meaning of the word, is a person for whom God suffices and needs nothing aside from God. This one says, "God is sufficient for me, I can forgo anything else." This one also has faith that, for whatever he was in need of and relinquished, God will send similar, if not better, things, and that, if He does not send anything, then it is because God knows this item is not essential. "It is impossible for God to know that I need an item and to withhold it from me; therefore, if He has not sent it, then He knows that I can do without it. If He has not sent it, then it is good." We have amazing examples of this in the lives of the monks. Two examples of this are St. Pijimi the Anchorite[212] and St. Moses the Anchorite.[213] They did not even have cooking utensils in their caves. They went out to the mountain and ate the grass off of the mountain and drank the water from the dew; they did not even need drinking vessels.

Release from Desires

If there is an item that your heart desires and you abstain from it, then this is true detachment. This detachment is not simply from this item, but rather, detachment from your heart's desire. The phrase, "my heart's desire," is not a monastic expression. Your heart should desire none other than God. Therefore, if your heart desires an item, then you must free it of this attachment. What then is monasticism? It is summed up by this phrase: "Release from all, and is

---

211 Cf. Mk 12:44

212 Cf. (El-Soriany 1993), 185–190. See also Sts. Timothy and Onnophrius (Vivian, Journeying into God: Seven Early Monastic Lives 1996) 172–187.

213 Ibid., 75–86.

bondage to the One."[214] Detachment is part of the "release from all." It is a manifestation of the "release from all." The one who possesses much and is not released of such, but rather adds more, fulfills the aphorism of Solomon the Sage: "The eye is not satisfied with seeing, nor the ear filled with hearing.... All the rivers run into the sea, yet the sea is not full."[215] Let your life in monasticism be, regarding material objects, a life of giving, and regarding spirituality, a life of receiving. The more you empty the material, the more God will fill you with the spiritual.

Also, the issue of detachment is sometimes connected with the virtue of contentment. Is this person content or not? One person rejoices in receiving many items, while another rejoices in giving away all the many items one has. Perhaps among the hindrances to detachment today are the many goods coming to the monastery, or the many gifts coming to a specific monk. People send many gifts, and the monastic cannot say no. If you cannot say no in taking, then distribute to others. I wish we would look in our cell every so often and "spring clean it" to relieve it of its burdens.

Believe me, one time I saw an amazing scene that would make a person keep nothing in the cell. A monk passed away and others entered his cell, and finished it off: the books went to the library, the clothes went to one person, the undergarments went to the workers, the black clothes went to another person, one person asked for the desk, another asked for the pot, another needed cups, and the utensils went to the kitchen. They finished off the cell that he had labored for a long time to gather items in before he departed in peace. If this is the case, he might as well have distributed these items himself and won his heavenly reward.

Lacking Possessiveness

St. Isaac teaches us a virtue higher even than poverty. Perhaps voluntary poverty is a monastic virtue, but there is a deeper

214 St. Isaac the Syrian (Miller 1984), 411.
215 Eccl 1:8, 7

virtue than poverty: being in need or impoverished.[216] The poor person might be content with being poor, having a little to live on, but "lacking" means you are in need of something and are unable to find it. This is even poorer than poverty. The person who is detached sets in the heart a very sensitive balance for necessities and excesses. What are necessities and excesses? The more detachment increases, the more one finds that items are excessive; and the more the love of possessions increases, the more inessential items enter into the category of necessities. This one becomes obliged to write letters making requests to laypeople, who send the items saying, "Poor monk!" Thus, the cell is further burdened, and if the possessions increase in the cell, the furnishings consequently increase. There is greater need for more closets, more drawers, more shelves, more luggage; it becomes an endless story. Perhaps one's possessions expand to more than one cell. When will this one become detached? When will you carry out the vow of poverty you took long ago? When will you be released from these bonds? When will you be sufficed, and when will you be released of possessions, not requesting any new items to add to what you currently have?

If you are a detached person, then you will not care about your appearance. Maybe the lowest quality clothing will suffice; you will not care to appear in a stylish fashion. The detached person does not make many requests. The more one dives into detachment, the fewer requests one makes; and if one reaches the depth of detachment, one makes absolutely no requests, always seeing what one has as more than what one needs.

We said that the virtue of detachment is a monastic virtue, but this virtue is for all. The verse that says "do not love the world or the things in the world"[217] takes us to the depth. It does not say, "Do not *possess* the things of the world," but do not even love them. Not only is possessing items beyond your needs a mistake, but even loving these items, even before possessing them, is wrong; in loving them, one has possessed them in the heart, even if they are not physically possessed in

---

216 (Miller 1984), 37–38.
217 1 Jn 2:15

one's personal dwelling.

The detached person does not envy those who possess, having no desire to have similar possessions. This one wants to be relieved of what one has. Christ tested the rich young man with the virtue of detachment. He told him, "Go, sell what you have and give to the poor ... and come, follow Me."[218] The rich young man was unable to detach himself from his wealth of possessions, so "he went away sorrowful."[219] The worst condition is for things not to be in your cell but in your heart and mind, where you think of them all day and all night. This is what truly troubles a person. The one who is detached from possessing items will not enter into a dispute, conflict, or debate with anyone. However, the one who is not detached might fight, saying, "This is mine. This is yours. This belongs to me!" These are not detached people.

Lacking Desires

Here we see that detachment is not only detachment from material possessions, but from everything, including desires, such as longing for certain jobs. If one person is tasked with a certain responsibility in the monastery and is then relieved of this responsibility, one gets upset, not wanting to be relieved of that duty. This one, instead of becoming detached, might become defiant and cause problems. If so, then this person has not yet been detached. Before you were ordained as a monk, did you have in mind that they would give you this specific responsibility in the monastery? The issue of detachment needs to extend to every aspect, so that no bonds would shackle you to anything.

You need to be detached from everything. Non-detachment, or attachment, contradicts the virtue of exile (withdrawal from the world). Why would one who feels like a stranger in the world possess anything in the world? "And the world is passing away, and the lust of it."[220] The virtue of exile helps a person along the virtue of detachment.

218 Mt 19:21
219 Mt 19:22
220 1 Jn 2:17

Likewise, not caring about tomorrow helps to attain the virtue of detachment. One might say, "I do not need this today, but I might need it tomorrow or the following day."

Another virtue that helps in attaining the virtue of detachment is love for God. If love for God reigns over your heart, you need nothing else to cheer you, feed you, or satiate you besides Him. Most certainly, for the non-detached person, the love of God has not filled the heart yet. This one's gaze at material possessions is not the look of one who has died to the world. There remain attachments that bind one to the world and materialistic things.

How easy it is for a person to say that this non-detachment is for the sake of others: to offer hospitality, to care for others, or to give to others. Here, I mention a catchy phrase of Abba Jacob: "It is better to be a guest than to give hospitality."[221]

We discussed many points of detachment, but the important thing is for us to apply them individually to our own weaknesses. Perhaps one is detached from material things but has not become detached from loving honor: "My honor! This word troubled me! My character!" See from where the enemy is withholding you, from what are you unable to detach, and win victory in this point, by the grace of our Lord Jesus Christ, to whom is due all glory forever. Amen.

---

221 (Ramfos 2000), 17.

PEACE IN THE LIFE OF A MONASTIC

In the Name of the Father, the Son, and the Holy Spirit,
One God. Amen.

Among the qualities that distinguish a monastic is a peaceful heart—peace continually reigns over a monastic's heart. This person is not disturbed, unsettled, anxious, upset, or irritated, and does not complain; but rather, this person lives in continuous peace of heart.

Peace Is a Gift from God

The Lord Christ gave us this peace, and we mention it in every liturgy, "My peace I leave with you, My peace I give to you."[222] He wants us to not only be filled with peace, but also to grant peace unto others; therefore, He said to His saintly apostles, "Whatever house you enter, first say, 'Peace to this house.'"[223] During the Divine Liturgy, the priest very frequently grants this peace to the congregation: "Peace be with you all."[224] The more internal peace a person has, the more one is able to perform God's work in calmness. Our teacher St. James says, "The fruit of righteousness is sown in peace."[225]

Losing Peace Is Unsettling

A monk who loses peace will be unable to carry out any work, either in the cell or outside the cell. He feels troubled. One first needs to be comforted, and thereafter one will be able to carry out spiritual work. A monk who loses peace becomes

222 Jn 14:27
223 Lk 10:5
224 (H and H 2007), 2, 18, 60.
225 Jas 3:18

unable to sit in his cell; a monk who loses peace cannot dwell in a cave. He becomes anxious and unsettled, and trapped in a tornado of thoughts from which that person seeks to escape. We would like each person to live in peace and assurance.

Peace Is a Gift of the Holy Spirit

Our teacher St. Paul said, "The fruit of the Spirit is love, joy, [and] peace."[226] These three go hand-in-hand. When you feel love for people, you will live in peace with people. When you feel love for God, you will live in peace with God and in both cases, you live in joy. One who lives in peace lives in joy, even if surrounded by hardships. By this peace of heart, one lives in hope that God will resolve problems and hardships. When you have this hope, then this verse in Romans applies to you: "Rejoicing in hope."[227]

Losing Peace Could Lead to Depression

The worst condition for a person to endure is to be surrounded by hardships, lose peace, and ultimately lose hope. Then, one would live in pain. This contributes to the psychological factors affecting people. This person is neither comfortable in the current condition, nor has hope that the situation will change. With the loss of peace comes the loss of joy; they always go hand-in-hand. This person ends up (mentally) despondent. This is not the sadness referred to in the Holy Bible in this verse: "By a sad countenance the heart is made better,"[228] rather, this is psychological depression.

Spiritual virtues are always interconnected. Do not think that when we refer to, "love, joy, and peace" that each virtue is exclusive of all other virtues. The three virtues are fully tied to each other. Each one of them could be a cause and/ or can have an effect on the other. Peace brings joy, and joy brings peace. Some people mistakenly think that monasticism

---

226 Gal 5:22
227 Rom 12:12
228 Eccl 7:3

is a life of depression, and that the goal set before monastics is the phrase repeated often in *The Paradise of the Holy Fathers*: "Sit in your cell and weep for your sins."[229]

Peace and Tears

I want to make a distinction between weeping and depression. A person might cry out of to joy, as when Jacob saw his son Joseph and "fell on his neck and wept on his neck a good while."[230] Also, when the temple was being rebuilt, the people "wept with a loud voice when the foundation of this temple was laid before their eyes. Yet many shouted aloud for joy, so that the people could not discern the noise of the shout of joy from the noise of the weeping of the people."[231] Tears differ from depression. Just because St. Arsenius wept,[232] it does not mean that his life was full of depression. A person might sorrow because of sins, but this is sorrow that leads to joy. Christ told His disciples, "You now have sorrow; but I will see you again and your heart will rejoice, and your joy no one will take from you."[233] When a person cries over sins, one feels comfort and therefore rejoices; this crying differs from depression and sorrow.

Peace is Apparent

When guests visit the monastery and find monks joyful, it gives them a good impression of the spiritual life. This shows that it leads to cheerfulness and joy. They should not come to find each person grimacing with troubled eyes, a frowning face, and trite expressions. What is the cause of this trouble? A true monastic finds no reason for sorrow. True sorrow should be held over sins, but, if you repent, then you should

---

229 (Budge 2008) Vol. II 45 {156}, 314 {618}, Vol I 228; (Ward, Desert Fathers 2003), 121 {16}, (Ward, Sayings 1984), 63 {1}, 126 {2}.
230 Gen 46:29
231 Ezek 3:12–13
232 (Ward, Sayings 1984), 18 {41}.
233 Jn 16:22

rejoice. There is nothing in this world that should be able to take away a monastic's peace. What in the monastery could possibly take away your peace? I can find nothing! What in monasticism could take away your peace? Nothing!

Sadness comes from outside, but joy is internal—in the heart. As the famous expression of St. Paul goes: "As sorrowful, yet always rejoicing; as poor, yet making many rich; as having nothing, and yet possessing all things."[234] The sorrow is external. People might look at the monastics and say: "Poor things, they have left the entire world. They have nothing, no family, and no children. They have none of the world's delights." The important thing is to make sure the external matters do not get to the inside. On the outside we may seem sorrowful, poor, and deprived, but on the inside we are joyful.

Peace in the Lord

A monastic should not have sorrow over being asked to change duties, leave the keys, or assume other responsibilities. To the monastic, it is all the same; always be happy. Why happy? Because your true joy is joy in the Lord, not in worldly affairs. If you have joy in worldly affairs, then you will be troubled if responsibilities are taken away. But if your joy is in the Lord, you will never be troubled because no one can take away the Lord: "Who shall separate us from the love of Christ?"[235] This is why St. Paul says, "Rejoice in the Lord always. Again I will say, rejoice!"[236] You should always be joyful; let peace reign over your heart. Do not be upset by anything. The only thing that should upset you is being separated from our Lord. You have the means to prevent this from happening; no one else can separate you from our Lord. St. Paul says, "Neither death nor life, nor angels nor principalities nor powers, nor things present nor things to come, nor height nor depth, nor any other created thing, shall be able to separate us from the

---

234 2 Cor 6:10
235 Rom 8:38
236 Phil 4:4

love of God which is in Christ Jesus our Lord."[237] Therefore, remain happy and let peace fill your heart.

Peace and Fear

One time, an Arian commander came to threaten St. Basil the Great:

> Modestus threatened impoverishment, exile, torture, death. Basil retorted that none of these threats frightened him: he had nothing to be confiscated except a few rags and a few books; banishment could not send him beyond the lands of God; torture had no terrors for a body already dead; death could only come as a friend to hasten his last journey home.[238]

Thus, absolutely no one is able to harm the children of God. St. John Chrysostom put it beautifully: "No one can harm the man who does not injure himself."[239] What can anyone do to you? Also, St. Augustine said, "I sat on the top of the world when I felt within that I did not desire anything or fear anything."[240] One who has desire has fear—fear of losing the desired object (if one already has it), or fear of not gaining it (if one does not already have it). One who wants nothing, naturally, fears nothing. When you feel in yourself that you desire nothing and fear nothing, you can trample the world under your feet. Regarding the phrase, "I want nothing," you could find a whole chapter full of many meditations in my book *The Release of the Spirit* titled: "I want nothing of the world."[241] You must have peace in your heart, peace with people, and peace with God. If you reach this peace, you will live with love towards everyone. Also, the Lord Christ said, "By this all will know that you are My disciples, if you have love for one another."[242]

---

237 Rom 8:38–39
238 (Library 1998), NPNF Series 2, Vol 8, 25–26.
239 Ibid., NPNF Series 1, Vol 9, 435.
240 (Shenouda III, Calmness 1997), 69.
241 (Shenouda III, The Release of the Spirit 1997), 88.
242 Jn 13:35

Peace and Community Life

Community interactions provide an opportunity for you to try yourself, overcome your weaknesses, and gain virtues. One time, a monk went to the abbot of the monastery asking to be released to go to another monastery. The abbot asked if anyone troubled him, to which he responded, "No, but I need to go attain virtues. Here, no one wrongs me, that I may forgive him; no one offends me, that I may pardon him; no one persecutes me, that I may endure him. So, where will I attain these virtues? I need to go to a place where I can attain virtues."[243] If you remain steadfast, and the community troubles come to you, then say, "Yes, this is where I will attain virtues." If someone upsets you, say, "Yes, God sent you to me so that I can attain the virtue of endurance."

Peace and Placidity

Sometimes, the way we deal with issues is what troubles us. The problem is not that people trouble us; the problem is that we are easily provoked. Like I said, trouble comes from your interaction, reaction, or response to a stimulus. If you are the irritable type, any word will irritate you. If you are not the irritable type, any word will pass. Believe me, I have found seculars who were much more easy-going than monks; if you tell them a word that might irritate a monk, they might laugh and respond with a joke, as if nothing happened.

I want to tell you something which St. Paul puts nicely: "O Corinthians! We have spoken openly to you, our heart is wide open. You are not restricted by us, but you are restricted by your own affections. Now in return for the same (I speak as to children), you also be open."[244] Be open-hearted. One time, I gave a group of people this illustration: if you take a small cup of water and place a speck of dirt in it, it will muddy the

---

243 (Beni-Suef Publication Committee 1977), 324.
244 2 Cor 6:11–13

entire cup, but if you place that same speck in the ocean, it will not muddy the ocean. The ocean will sink it down to its depth and give you fresh water. Now the question is, "Are you a cup, or are you an ocean?" Are you the type who loses your temper by words? If you say that the words are irritating, even if they are, are you the type of person who is easily angered or not? If you are easily angered, then the problem is not in the words, but in you. Try to remedy this issue within yourself, and thus, become placid. This is a lengthy process; I wrote a book titled *Anger in Spiritual Wars*, and if you read it, you will find much information on this issue. Ask yourself, "Why am I angered? Is it because this person hurt my pride? Am I the type who cares about honor? Perhaps the problem is in me if I care about honor." I will tell you a story:

When a brother asked St. Macarius how to be saved, he told the monk to go to the cemetery and insult the dead; when the brother reported that he had done as he was told, St. Macarius then told him to go praise the dead. When the monk returned again, St. Macarius asked him, "Did they answer you?" When the monk said "No," St. Macarius drove home his point: "You know how you insulted them and they did not reply, and how you praised them and they did not speak; so you too if you wish to be saved you must do the same and become a dead man. Like the dead, take no account of either the scorn of men or their praises, and you can be saved."[245]

Likewise, since you have died to the world, you should not rejoice in praise, nor be troubled by insult. If an insult comes and you endure it, say, "I have a reward in the Kingdom." If someone insults you, does this insult diminish your personality? Does it affect your monasticism? Does it take away your adoption by God? It has no effect. "You also be open."[246]

Christ said, "You shall be witnesses to Me."[247] He did not say that you should play security guard, but that you should simply witness to the truth. If others accept the truth, that is

245 (Vivian, Saint Macarius the Spiritbearer: Coptic Texts Relating to Saint Macarius the Great 2004), 22.
246 2 Cor 6:13
247 Acts 1:8

wonderful; if not, so be it. Will you force people? Even our Lord does not force people to do good deeds.

Peace and Gentleness

If you are in a position of responsibility and others around you are hindering the work, what should you do? Explain the correct method to them. If they accept, great; if they do not listen, then go to the person in charge in the monastery and explain the correct procedure. Explain that if it is carried out in another way it will not work, and be relieved of the blame. If people are upset because of the truth, do not be troubled by this. If someone is upset by the truth, this is not your sin, nor is it your responsibility for this. People were also upset with Christ because He spoke the truth. What is important is the approach you use in explaining your point. Tell people the correct method without hurting their feelings, without making them feel ignorant. Personally, I consult people of intelligence, experience, and knowledge in many issues, and I do not get upset. And if they tell me that I did something that was wrong, I stop. Who wants to do something that is wrong? Your method of explaining should not be irritating. The way that you relay information should not be hurtful. The saints say, "Obedience and lowliness gives men power over wild beasts."[248] The more convincing your argument is, the less people are troubled; rather, they will be pleased to learn and benefit from you.

Peace and Community Success

If you do not express your opinion, but rather isolate yourself from the community, driving all matters aside in order to avoid community friction, this cannot be called success in the community; rather a person should enter the community, become exposed to its trials, and succeed. One time, a monk went to the abbot asking permission to go into

---

248 Saint Anthony (Ward, Sayings 1984), 8 {36}. Lowliness replaces abstinence, for consistency with the Arabic.

isolation. The abbot asked the reason and the monk explained that he was troubled by the brethren in the community. The abbot responded, "If you are unable to endure the troubles of the brethren in the community, how will you endure the troubles of the devils in solitude?"[249] During your time in the community, you are testing yourself to see if you can bear with people. Do you lose your peace? Do you hate people? Or do you try to avenge oneself? If you try to isolate yourself in order not to engage in these troubles, you are likened to a person who refuses to take an exam for fear of failing. The result is that you will not graduate. The correct action is for a person to take the exam and pass. It is easy to sit alone and not make mistakes. Neither will the devil leave you; he will give you even more thoughts than people would, to the point that you will leave your cell saying, "It is better to deal with people than to deal with this mental warfare." Take the test and succeed.

All glory and honor is due to our God forever. Amen.

---

249 Cf. (Chryssavgis 2003), 70.

TIME

In the Name of the Father, the Son, and the Holy Spirit,
One God. Amen.

Monastic Time

Today I want to speak with you about the monk's time. To what extent do you benefit from or utilize your time? Time could be on your side, or it could be against you. The difference between the most saintly monk and the most negligent monk is your use of time.

Your time should be spent in spiritual labor. The more you employ your time for spiritual labor, the deeper your relationship with God develops, and the further your monastic life is refined and strengthened. A person might object, "I am busy, I have work," but I would respond, "Benefit from befriending the night." The one who befriends the night is able to behave suitably during the day. We are now in winter and the nights are long; you could use the night for spiritual labor.

The psalm says, "Behold, bless the Lord, all you servants of the Lord, who by night stand in the house of the Lord. Lift up your hands."[250] St. Isaac says, "The night is set apart to engage in prayer."[251] We hear that St. Arsenius spent the night in prayer. He would pray facing the east as the sun was setting behind him and would wait until it appears before him.[252] The Lord Christ spent "all night in prayer."[253] The nights have no preoccupations, appointments, chatter with people, or other hindrances, so try to benefit from them. Daylight assists in reading or writing, meanwhile, nighttime could be utilized in prayer: your own prayers, psalms, meditations, retreats with yourself and with God, and in hymns or praises. All these are feasible in the darkness. Try to benefit from the night.

---

250 Ps 134:1–2
251 Cf. (Miller 1984), 308, 370–372.
252 Cf. (Ward, Sayings 1984), 14; (Ramfos 2000), 93.
253 Lk 6:12

Remarks Concerning Time

Set an organized schedule; one who does not set a schedule sometimes becomes disoriented.

Train yourself to maintain spiritual labor during your work responsibilities in the monastery—for example, secret prayers during work. This can be possible if you train yourself to pray during walking, working, and during your encounters with others. This will train your heart to be continually preoccupied with God. Preoccupy your heart especially with what you have memorized, your psalms, and short repeated prayers, and then your heart will unceasingly be praying.

You should give God the beginning of your day, the first fruits of your time, and (as much as possible) your best time. Make God the first person you speak with during the day, and do not become preoccupied with anything else. If your time is tight, make him the first person you address and the first with whom you are absorbed, even if it is just for a short period.

If you are able to relax or sleep for an hour or two during the day, it could help you keep vigil at night. If you spend the whole day working, you might come at night to find yourself exhausted.

You have to place a principle before you: your time primarily belongs to God, it does not belong to you. When you consecrated your life to God, your entire time became God's and you cannot convince yourself otherwise. All your time belongs to God.

Here I want to tell you that your time is your life. If you waste your time, then you have wasted your life. What is your life more than time? Your time should be for your spiritual development, and as time passes by, you should be building yourself more than previously. Therefore, ask yourself, "To what level have I developed?"

There are saints who flourished in a short period of time because they seriously took advantage of time in their spiritual life. Therefore, they were raised to the levels of spiritual guidance while they were still young. Perhaps, I could mention here the examples of St. Theodore (the disciple of St. Pachomius) and St. John the Short, of whom it was said that he "has all Scetis hanging from his little finger."[254] Both were spiritual guides to the entire monastery while still in their youth. I could also mention a youth who matured immensely in the monastic life, who is unmatched: St. Misael the Anchorite. He came to the monastery when he was 14, and after three or four years, when he was about 18, he became an anchorite. This is because he took the matter very seriously, and utilized every moment of his time.

Another example of youths who flourished rapidly at a young age would be St. Maximus and St. Dometius. They are always portrayed as young men, to the point where Dometius's beard had not grown. They seriously profited from their time, and did not allow any moment of time to pass by without continuous spiritual work, which yielded a result. One could also examine the history of the saints, and see the rest of the saints who quickly flourished at a young age, because they benefited from their time.

Time Consuming Objects

What wastes your time? Perhaps work. I told you that the remedy for this is the night; and prayer during work. If you are successful in spiritual labor, the monastery could possibly help relieve you from some of the work responsibilities, such that you would be dedicated to spiritual labor. The monastery could not relieve a person whom it sees running east and west, talking all day long. They would say, "Will we release this person to chatter, run around, and talk?" If they could relieve a person who is successful in spiritual labor, then the monastery would take that person's blessing.

Among the items that waste time are friendships and spending too much time in speaking about what is beneficial and non-beneficial (more so in what is non-beneficial). It is rare for two people to sit together and build each other or

254 (Ward, Sayings 1984), 93.

speak of what is mutually beneficial. Try in your conversations with your friends to make your sessions spiritual, or revolve around a spiritual subject.

Among the hindrances is sleep. One who finds nothing to do in his cell might fall asleep. The danger of sleep is that if it exceeds its limit it can become an opportunity for thoughts. One needs to be wise, knowing the body's precise needs. Are you truly exhausted and need to sleep, or is it just laziness?

Among the items that waste time are thoughts. Thoughts can take a person into several places, sometimes frivolous or non-spiritual. It is easy for the enemy to portray the simple issues as crucial and needing immediate attention, such that a person sitting in his cell might think of work: "What will we do and how will we do it?" This is a waste of time. A person needs to control the thoughts in order to know how to benefit from the time in the cell. Certainly, if there is no positive spiritual work, there will be an opportunity for thoughts.

Another person might become occupied in his cell with many petty pastimes; the object is simply time consumption: arrange the cell, organize paperwork, clean, work any handiwork, cook, make a cup of tea, or go speak with someone. Often these items do not come to mind except when this person begins spiritual work; one replaces the other.

Among the items that waste time is for the mind to replay what it saw during the day. It finds audiovisual flashbacks of the entire past: discussions, images, actions, meetings, and conversations, as well as the mind's consequent inferences— this consumes a great amount of time.

In addition, paying attention to the news and following up with it consumes time. Certainly it takes time to gather the news, and then to replay it mentally.

There are also other personal hindrances specific to each person.

My advice would be that it is important for each person to benefit from time as much as possible. You must have spiritual work inside and outside your cell; and in both you must be organized and punctual. You should be committed to certain spiritual principles that must be followed, and respect your monastic time. Believe me, if you know how to benefit from your time, the result is twofold: remaining in your cell and not leaving it (because you are happy with the time spent there), and silence and calmness when meeting people (because you are engaged in internal work, which does not provide the opportunity for speaking and having a conversation). The opposite is also true: if you have no work in your cell and do not know how to use your time, you will come out to talk to every passerby. The person who has no work will chatter and is in no way able to remain silent. This is why you should always engage your mind, your thoughts, and your mouth in unceasing prayer. Try to appreciate the value of your time.

Various Time Engaging Spiritual Labors

Prayer: this is divided into categories: church, psalms, personal prayers from the heart containing your supplications to God, short memorized prayers which you repeat continously, and perhaps some memorized prayers of the prophets and saints (either from the Holy Bible or from prayer books). The more prayer involves meditation, the longer it takes. Sometimes one person might pray quickly without feeling so as to finish prayers, feeling no link or relationship with God; it is simply fulfilling an obligation. Try to pray slowly, calmly, with understanding, and with meditation, blend the prayer with your feelings and your spirit, and then it will certainly take time. Thus, you will have gained the lost time. Train yourself continually to resist lost time; sit with yourself and ask yourself, "What is wasting my time?"

Singing: praising and psalmody have a great impact on the soul.

Reading: the Holy Bible, hagiography (the lives of the saints), spiritual and ascetical books, and any additional works of interest to expand your religious knowledge.

Meditation: either in a verse in the Bible, hagiography, God's characteristics, or any spiritual topic.

Metanoias (prostrations) should be accompanied with prayers; every prostration should have its own prayer. They should be prayed using a prayer rope, so that your preoccupation is not with counting, but rather with your prayers. They could all be around one topic (with many details), or around several topics.

Writing, Translating, or Transcribing.

I would like to make another point: if you find that your time is tight, compensate the shortness with depth; a short amount of time with great depth is better than much time with no depth. Notice that the thief with only one sentence gained that promise of salvation (that he would be in Paradise); likewise, the publican prayed one sentence. People with little time who pray deeply, have found they have benefited and their hearts were spiritually filled to satisfaction, as a result of the depth of their prayer.

May Glory be to God forever. Amen.

HARDHEARTEDNESS

In the Name of the Father, the Son, and the Holy Spirit,
One God. Amen.

I would like to speak with you about an important point in a person's spiritual life connected to one's sins. The Holy Bible continually maintains that the obstacle hindering any person's repentance is hardheartedness. St. Paul the vvvv says in the epistle to the Hebrews: "Today, if you will hear his voice, do not harden your hearts."[255] Non-responsiveness to God's voice inside the heart is caused by hardness within the heart. The gentle heart is one that is easily affected and fast responding, the slightest signal from God makes it rush to Him immediately, without delay. Believe me, even some of the hearts that fall prey to desires, and are moved by bodily and worldly desires, perhaps have more gentleness and emotion in responding to God's voice than the hard, difficult hearts.

Gentle Hearts

I will give you amazing examples of people who might have seemed difficult to other people, but were very gentle in responding to God. Take for example Matthew the tax collector (tax collectors have a reputation for being hard and difficult), he did not need from Christ except the simple word, "Follow Me,"[256] and he left everything and followed Him, although he had financial responsibilities at the tax office. Take someone like Zacchaeus the chief tax collector, perhaps in the eyes of people he was a cruel person, but he could not delay when Christ told him, "Zacchaeus, make haste and come down."[257]

These quick-responding hearts do not contain cruelty that prevents the way to God. Christ told Peter and Andrew,

---

255 Heb 3:8, 15; 4:7
256 Mt 9:9
257 Lk 19:5

"Follow Me,"[258] they quickly left the boat and their entire lives and followed Him. Peter, in his sin, by one glance from Christ, or by simply hearing the sound of the cock's crow "went out and wept bitterly."[259]

These souls do not need God to labor much, the slightest spiritual work, or work of grace, finds a response from them; as for hard hearts, no matter what God does, there is absolutely no response. One could read a spiritual book full of moving phrases with absolutely no impact, or hear a sermon with no effect, attend a liturgy again with no response, confess with no effectiveness, and enter the church and leave exactly the same, unaffected; as if God is chiseling on a rock. These are hard hearts.

Perhaps accidents occur; to one person the slightest accident feels like the voice of God calling and so responds, while to another many accidents occur, sicknesses, trials, and tragedies without any effect, without a response—there is hardness within the heart; therefore, He says, "Today, if you will hear His voice, do not harden your hearts."[260] The spiritual person hears God's voice, even from afar and says, "Lord I am coming." See what the Shulamite says, "The voice of my beloved! Behold, he comes leaping upon the mountains, skipping upon the hills,"[261] He is coming from afar, and yet she is able to distinguish His voice. She is able to distinguish it; even if she is sleeping, she is able to distinguish it. Her heart is alert.

Souls Unaffected, Neither by Love nor by Adversity

These sensitive souls hear God's voice, but on other souls God has no effect. Neither God's love nor His punishment affect them or draw them. I will give you an example of each case. God's love did not affect or draw the children of Israel in the wilderness. He split the Red Sea for them to pass through, He saved them from slavery, He led them by the cloud in the

258 Mt 4:19
259 Mt 26:75
260 Heb 3:8; 15; 4:7
261 Song 2:8

daytime and the pillar of fire by night, He erupted for them water from a rock, He sent them the Manna and quails. All these works of love had no effect on them; they worshipped the golden calf when Moses delayed on the mountain. God's love has no affect on these hard hearts. To contrast, there is a sensitive person who, at the slightest expression of love from God, says, "God, I'm embarrassed from You, Your love shames me, I am at Your feet." Some souls are neither affected by love, nor by adversity.

Another example is Pharaoh. How many were the plagues? After each one he proclaimed, "I have sinned ... Now therefore, please forgive my sin only this once, and entreat the Lord your God ... I will let you go."[262] Then, as soon as the trial passed and relief came, Pharaoh forgot what happened, and returned to his former hardness. There is hardness in his heart; therefore the Bible speaks of how "the heart of Pharaoh was hard."[263] The plagues had no impact on him because his heart was hard internally, unable to respond to God's voice.

Let us see an example of this: the stony ground, on which seeds fell, was unable to bring forth fruit or vegetate; the farmer planted but there was no response. The difference between the sensitive hearts which respond quickly and the hard hearts with which neither love nor discipline work, is like the difference between the tender branch and the dry branch. You could prune the tender branch as you wish, you could turn it, fix it, change its direction, and it responds because it is malleable in your hand; this is impossible with the dry branch, if you apply pressure to it, it breaks without yielding any result. There is hardness in the heart internally, which makes it non-responsive.

As for the hardhearted person, as Solomon the Wise said, "Though you grind a fool in a mortar with a pestle along with crushed grain, yet his foolishness will not depart from him";[264] he remains the same, his heart remains unchanged. Our Lord gave us an example of this in His reproach to His people: "All day long I have stretched out My hands to a disobedient and

262 Ex 9:27, 28; Ex 10:17
263 Ex 9:35
264 Prov 27:22

contrary people";[265] it is amazing that God spread His hands out towards a people who do not respond to Him, therefore He called them "stiff-necked,"[266] cruel, violent, hardhearted.

We also saw this hardheartedness in the days of Christ, from people to whom Christ performed innumerable miracles of healing, exorcisms, resurrections, and unprecedented miracles, and yet they concluded by the phrase, "Crucify Him, crucify Him,"[267] because there is hardhearted non-responsiveness internally.

Admonition, advice, rebuke, or spiritual means do not work with everyone; consequently Christ says, "Behold, I stand at the door and knock. If anyone hears My voice and opens the door, I will come in";[268] some might refuse to open to Him due to their hardheartedness, because they are non-responsive internally, regardless of the external call. These people remind us of Abraham the Patriarch's response to the rich man (in the story of the rich man and Lazarus) who asked him to send Lazarus to his household to testify to them; Abraham responded, "Neither will they be persuaded though one rise from the dead."[269]

The Difference Between Saints and Sinners

As for the gentle heart, one that does not use cruelty with God, it is distinguished by continuous tears in the eyes, repentance in the heart, a readiness to return, and and easily being affected. The difference between the saints and the sinners is not that saints do not sin (the Bible explained the sins of the saints), but that when saints sin they are quickly moved and return, as soon as they become aware of their mistakes their tears flow and they long for a life with God. This is the difference; it does not mean a sinless person. We all sin; no one is infallible. David the prophet sinned, his sins were hideous, but once he became aware of his sin he

---

265 Rom 10:21
266 Ex 32:9; 33:3, 5; 34:9; Deut 9:6, 13
267 Lk 23:21; Jn 19:6
268 Rev 3:20
269 Lk 16:31

displayed his remorse remarkably, his tears abundantly flowed, and drenched his couch with his tears[270] profusely. In taking a census of the people, when the prophet alerted him, he said, "I have done very foolishly ... I have sinned greatly ... Please let me fall into the hand of the Lord, for His mercies are very great; but do not let me fall into the hand of man."[271] This is a very sensitive person, his heart has no hardness, he might deviate or stray, but he is not cruel; he is quickly awakened when called and is not obstinate with God; his fall might be out of weakness, but it would not be out of treachery, and if he is called, he responds quickly. Our Lord seeks these souls, God never ever desires severity, therefore, He said, "Blessed are the merciful, for they shall obtain mercy."[272]

God's Reproof to Sinners

One who is rigid in the relationship with God is more likely to be rigid in relationships with others. If one does not respond to God's voice, one will not respond to a human voice. In His Holy Bible, our Lord admonishes us alongside His people who rejected Him, saying: "What more could have been done to My vineyard that I have not done in it? Why then, when I expected it to bring forth good grapes, did it bring forth wild grapes?"[273] The cruel heart which brings about no result, despite all the spiritual means offered to it, is like a sick person who does not respond to all different types of medical treatments. You offer it pills with no result, you offer it injections with no result, you offer it electrotherapy with no result, and so forth, and therefore it is labeled non-responsive.

One who responds to treatment shows improvement, no matter how subtle, which means that there is hope. This is not a hard heart; the hard heart is like a rock. Our Lord complained of the hardhearted: "Be astonished, O heavens,

270 Ps 6:6
271 1 Chr 21:8, 13
272 Mt 5:7
273 Is 5:4

at this, and be horribly afraid."[274] Our Lord is able to forgive everyone as long as you respond to His voice, but the hardhearted have a different stance with God. Our Lord does not like hardheartedness, nor does He like pride. He could forgive, but pride and hardheartedness—see what the Bible says: "God resists the proud,"[275] He *resists*; He did not say this of any other type of sin. Therefore I wish that a person would try to gain tenderness of heart and stay away from hardheartedness!

Stubbornness Leads to Hardheartedness

Perhaps hardheartedness results from continuous obstinacy; continual rejection produces hardness inside the heart. In the beginning of their relationship with sin, a person might be afraid or ashamed, the heart or conscience might be disturbed internally, but if one silences it, then engages and continues indulging in sin, then hardheartedness comes to the point that the sin is committed without shame.

One who is engaged in sin, who has no prior experience of life with God, is perhaps shaken by the spiritual means at the first experience of God: the Bible is influential, the liturgy is influential, the hymns are influential, and the sermons are influential. It becomes most painful if a person loses these influences. When the ears are no longer good transmitters to the heart, one hears without influence. The hardest thing is for the verses in Hebrews [Chapter] 6 to happen: "For the earth which drinks in the rain that often comes upon it, and bears herbs useful for those by whom it is cultivated, receives blessing from God; but if it bears thorns and briars, it is rejected and near to being cursed, whose end is to be burned."[276] It drank much water, but brought forth no result, because there is hardheartedness. The land became stony in its depth; it became non-responsive. This is a very difficult condition.

The person distant from spiritual sustenance is not in the

---

274 Jer 2:12
275 Jas 4:6; 1 Pet 5:5
276 Heb 6:7–8

worst condition (through spiritual sustenance this one might reform), but rather the one who lives with spiritual means and yet produces no result. This is like a person who develops tolerance for a certain medicine, to the point that it ceases to have any effect. This is the very difficult case. If you try talking to this person, the response would be, "We have heard much of these sermons," they have lost their effect. The heart has become stone.

Examine Yourself

If you find that you have entered this realm, beware; if you find that the liturgies, the hymns, the spiritual words you heard or read that were influential now have no influence on you, beware. Fear that you might have started a transformation towards hardheartedness, because one of the manifestations of hardheartedness is dryness, spiritual drought, and not being influenced by spirituality or spiritual means. Seek out the reasons for this hardness in your heart, and try to remedy them. See what is hardening your heart internally. Is there a beloved sin, a wicked relationship, a wrong understanding of spirituality, sinful behaviors, or obstacles to the spiritual path before you that have hardened your heart? Search and remedy. Our Lord knows that you could sin, but if you sin and your heart is tender, the slightest sound from God would awake you, bring you back, and help you repent, but if you become desensitized to sin or sin became your second nature, then your heart becomes hard. One of its signs is also that a person neither exercises self rebuke, nor accepts rebuke from others.

Glory be to God forever. Amen.

VALUES

In the Name of the Father, the Son, and the Holy Spirit,
One God. Amen.

Today I want to speak with you about values, or evaluating
matters. A person's personality and life path are determined
by values. The difference among people are a result of their
different evaluation of matters, their understanding of things,
and the way they go about judging matters.

The Value of Money

Take a simple example: money. One person might spend
money and consider it generosity, while another considers it
squandering. The one who considers it squandering will not
spend money, while the one who considers it generosity will.
The one who sees that money will not remain forever, that
it will not be taken [with them] to heaven, nor will be taken
when leaving the world would say, "I will store up treasures
for myself in heaven,"[277] but the one who considers money
the support source here on earth would say, "A good penny
comes in handy on a rainy day." This one does not depend on
God for support, and is not willing to spend anything. To one,
money is a god—one that is worshiped—while to another it
is a means through which one gains friends on earth and wins
a place in heaven. According to a person's valuations, matters
are determined.

To one money is a goal, while to another it has no value and
could in no way be a goal. According to a person's viewpoint
on this issue one's life path is determined. St. Anthony, the
first monk, considered money worthless, therefore he was
able to sell all his possessions, whereas, the rich ruler to
whom the Lord spoke went away sad. He could not part with
money because to him it had total value—to the point that he

---

277 Cf. Lk 12:33

would not listen to advice from Christ Himself. Who would meet Christ and go away sad? Money had value in his heart.

Valuing the Whole World

The whole world, what is its value? To one person, the world is everything (especially to those who do not believe in eternity, such as the communists or existentialists), while to some people it is petty and rubbish, as St. Paul says, "I have suffered the loss of all things, and count them as rubbish, that I may gain Christ."[278] He not only suffered loss, thinking he had lost something of value, but he lost it while considering it rubbish, trash, valueless. A person's viewpoint of things is what determines the personality. Why does a monastic come to monasticism? Because at one point the world was considered like a trashcan, rubbish, therefore one was able to become a monastic, but, if the world had value, one would never have come to the monastery.

Valuing Worldly Pleasures

Solomon the Wise went through both stages. At one point worldly pleasures had a very high value in his life. The delight of his life was world pleasure, therefore he said, "Whatever my eyes desired I did not keep from them."[279] He made sure to have orchards, houses, possessions, gold, silver, maidens, wives, and all that could delight secular people. Thereafter, Solomon found that "all is vanity and grasping for the wind"[280]—one who is trying to grasp wind in his hand would catch nothing. As for Solomon, his perception changed, his values changed, and his valuation of matters changed. Orchards, money, women, eating, and drinking all had their place in his heart; yet, when he started exercising abstinence they lost their value.

---

278 Phil 3:8
279 Eccl 2:10
280 Eccl 1:14

Renewal of the Mind

This is the point the Apostle is making: "Be transformed by the renewing of your mind"[281]—one's mind is renewed. We take the renewal in baptism (the renewal of our nature), but the renewal of the mind is a continual process in our lives. For one to have a new mind and new thoughts, the thoughts and the outlook on matters also need to change. What is your outlook on matters? What is your understanding? How do you evaluate, or value matters? This is what determines your personality and your behavior in life. To you, does the world have weight, or is it weightless? Do life pleasures have value? Do world possessions have value? Does worldly status have value to you? What is the extent of your dealings with the world and people in the world? Do you think of what you will be in this world? Or what you will be in another world? In order to direct our attention to the correct valuation of the world, the church chose a verse from the first epistle of St. John to always be placed at the end of the Catholic Epistle in every liturgy: "Do not love the world or the things in the world ... the world is passing away, and its lust";[282] from here came the virtue of "dying to the world." One is unable to live the notion of dying to the world unless the world has no value in their eyes. But of course a secular person would ask: "Die to the world, how?!" All their effort is to have a name in the world! One needs to have a correct perception of matters. The more correct our perception is, the more we are able to walk accordingly. When Solomon's perception was changed, only then was he able to repent.

Valuing Holy Labor

Also, for Solomon we need to see what labor was: "I looked on all the works that my hands had done and on the labor in which I had toiled; and indeed all was vanity."[283] One might ask, "Does this mean we should not labor in life? Wouldn't

281 Rom 12:2
282 1 Jn 2:15–17
283 Eccl 2:11

this lead to disinterest or negligence?" There are two kinds of labor: holy labor and vain labor. Vain labor is a person's labor for worldly matters. Why is it vain? Because it ends with the end of these matters, or, because it is for vain matters. As for holy labor, it is for God, for eternity, for the kingdom of God in your heart, and for spreading the kingdom on earth. Here the Book says, "Each one will receive his own reward according to his own labor"[284]—this is holy labor. Everyone, ask yourself if your labor is holy labor or vain labor. The devil labors for the destruction of souls; his labor is vain. Many people labor for matters that absolutely do not deserve labor—vain matters that last for a specified time and then end.

Valuing Vain Labor

Depending on a person's valuation of labor and rest, one might choose to labor or not to labor. There is a person who flees from labor, and there is one who chases after labor, knowing its rewards. One labors in prayer, in worship, in prostrations, in fasts, and in subduing the body, while another labors for fame, for money, for knowledge, for status, for sports (wanting to be the world champion in running, perhaps, or maybe not). What is labor? What labor do you want? Solomon found that all his labor was for money, fame, grandeur, and bodily desire. Afterwards he found that all this labor was in vain. Therefore, there is a lingering question before us: "What is labor according to our father Solomon the Wise?" Vain materials perish and cannot remain forever. What remains with you in heaven is not vain because it will remain with you, but whatever ends with the end of the world is vain.

---

284 1 Cor 3:8

Properly Valuing the Whole World

What is this whole world! What is this whole world, with all its continents, its past, present, and future, what does it amount to? Nothing! I like one of the scholars who said the following statement: "When I was a child I saw myself in comparison to the world as a small speck of sand on an endless beach of an endless ocean." So what if someone lives in such-and-such a city, and this city is part of this specific country, and this country is a small part of this specific continent, and this continent is a small part of planet Earth, and planet Earth is a small part of the millions of innumerable planets. What would that be? It is nothing.... What does this person come out to be? He says: "When I was a child I saw myself in comparison to the world as a small speck of sand on an endless beach of an endless ocean, but now I know that I am the endless ocean and the whole world is a small speck of sand on my beach"; what is this world! One who sits to think of the world finds that it is frivolous. If you asked him, "What is the world," he would say, "A small speck of sand on my beach," and "What is your endless beach," "This is the beach leading to eternity." If you find yourself as the image and likeness of God, then what does this world amount to? With all that it has of noise, struggles, desires, status, what does the world amount to? Nothing. This is a person's valuation of the world.

Valuing True Holy Labor

Solomon labored to do all this, and then found that all this labor was in vain: what are lusts, what are desires, what is the body, what does it amount to? Nothing! Does this lead to indifference? No. It leads us to true labor for matters that do not fade away. What does that mean? St. Paul said, "We do not look at the things which are seen, but at the things which are not seen. For the things which are seen are temporary, but the things which are not seen are eternal."[285] Everything you see is temporary; it remains for a while and then ends. The person

---

285 2 Cor 4:18

who does not value the world does not labor for the world—
neither for gaining the world nor for losing the world. This
one would ask you, "What is this world? Nothing," and would
turn into, as the Book puts it, "Those who use this world as
not misusing it."[286] You need to be faithful whatever your
circumstances are in the world, faithful over the little that you
do in the world, and therefore you will be entrusted by God
over much—eternal life. Faithfulness is not out of love for
the world, but out of love for faithfulness, purity of heart,
and perfection, such that one is faithful in every condition.

Valuing Comfort

Then we come to ask, "What is comfort and what is labor?
What is your valuation of comfort, and what is your valuation
of labor?" There is one person to whom comfort is bodily
comfort, physical rest, not overexertion; to another it is
comfort of mind, internal comfort, ease of mind, not wanting
to be inconvenienced; another's comfort is comfort of heart
and its desires—fulfilling wants and desires; to another it
is a comfortable conscience, having a clear conscience—
considering all the previous comforts valueless; and to another
true comfort is eternal comfort, for which one pursues, even
if that means laboring with all the power in the world in
order to attain that comfort. If a person departs from this
world they say that this person rested in peace, meaning they
found comfort—comfort from vain labor and entering into
true comfort. According to the person's understanding of
comfort, one's personality and life are determined.

A person might come at night saying: "I'm tired, I want to
sleep and rest."

But the mind responds, "How could you rest when you
have not prayed, you have to stay awake and pray."

"But I'm tired," [the person says to themself]

"Physically," [the mind responds], "but you will have rest
of mind and heart concerning your eternity when you pray."

If one cares only for the bodily comfort, then there will

---

286 1 Cor 7:31

be no prayer: "Lord, You know I'm tired today, let us get past the issue of prayer just today, and I'll make it up to You tomorrow"; but, if we seek comfort of the conscience, then there will be vigil, even if it requires labor. Here the perception of comfort changes. What is comfort? People use the same expressions but the valuation and understanding of the expressions differ from one person to another.

Valuing Comfort

I will give you another example of comfort: one father finds all his comfort in pleasing his son, and no matter how hard he labors, he rejoices in labor because he has comforted his son. So, to him true comfort is his child's joy. A servant, one who serves God in the church, finds her greatest comfort in comforting those whom she serves: if she is able to lead people to repentance, to solve problems, to bring some to church, or bring some to confession, then she rejoices. This is her comfort. Why? Because a specific problem has been resolved. Someone in the service had a big problem and it was resolved. She will be so happy to have found comfort, although she might return physically and mentally exhausted from debating and negotiating with people, yet this is her understanding of comfort.

Negative Values of Comfort

Some people only find comfort in destroying others—to them this is the greatest comfort. Take for example an avenger, if he does not take vengeance for his murdered brother or father he could not find comfort. When he does take vengeance, only then he is comfortable. "Why are you comfortable?" "Because I killed so-and-so." This is his comfort; this is where he finds his comfort. Some people are this way; they find their comfort in another's labor, like, some marital problems or disputes within a family. One student might find comfort in surpassing another student, not out of love for excelling, but out of a desire to surpass this specific person, to devastate this person. Or a young lady whose comfort is to overcome a young man known to be religious, whom none were able to defeat, but she was able to defeat him and would rejoice, this is her comfort. Satan's greatest delight is to destroy a person, dragging him or her to Hades, if he does, he is very happy—as the heavens rejoice over one sinner who repents, the devils rejoice over one who sins. The understanding of comfort differs from one person to another. We all understand comfort, but what is the meaning of comfort in the mind of each person? What is the meaning of comfort? One is comfortable for overcoming another and is pleased; in contrast, one has comfort in being able to please another. See how these two comforts are very different! The perception of comfort differs from one person to another. The whole world differs, with all its millions of occupants, as a result of the variation of people's values.

Valuing Power

Take power for example, what is your valuation of power? One person considers power the ability to overcome another person, to overcome and be a hero, while another understands power as overcoming oneself, internally. The Wise [Solomon] says, "He who rules his spirit [is better] than he who takes a city"[287]—so, what is power? Is it physical power like wrestlers and boxers? Is it mental power, like one who devises a plot and succeeds, even if it ruins people in the process? One would tell you, "This person's brain is devilish," and he boasts of such a mind, "He is such a devil"—and boasts of this powerful mentality, even if this mind ruins others. To another, power is internal, inside the heart, inside the self, inside the thoughts; the power to overcome internally, overcome sin, overcome Satan; power to subdue the self; power to control or steer the will; this is this person's viewpoint of power. This is the valuation of matters: what is power?

---

287 Prov 16:32

Valuing Physical Power

Some adolescents think that power is physical power, therefore their heroes are physically strong champions; they even call it: "Power lifting." "This is power, to lift some weights, throw the shot put, win at wrestling, wrestle a bull (in the Olympics, they used to wrestle bulls), win at boxing. This is power, Samsonite power—pick up a door, hit some people—this is power!" To another, the perception of power is: the power of speech—one can say a word that "avails much" (Jas 5:16); mental power; will power; spiritual power—spirits strong enough to overcome other spirits. If you find a person with a powerful spirit, a devil passing by will flee because it sees a powerful spirit before it. What is your perception of power? Is power overcoming yourself, or overcoming others?

Valuing Bodily Power

Is power found in your spirit or in your body? The matter is one's perception and valuation; based on the perceptions and valuations to matters a person's life is shaped. Take the body and spirit for example; what is your valuation of the body and spirit. One person's whole concern is the body, only caring for the body: how it lives, is healthy, is empowered, is fed, is delighted with all kinds of pleasures, such as pleasures of the senses for example, in eating and drinking; There are people who are like that. A person who is struggling in the spiritual life considers the body [akin to] a sin to struggle against with full might. A spiritual person sees the body as a temple of the Holy Spirit—"Do you not know that your body is the temple of the Holy Spirit who is in you"[288]—and also looks at the bodies of others in the same way, and therefore does not fall into bodily sins. This one sanctifies the body as a temple of God, always seeing the verse that says, "Glorify God in your body and in your spirit, which are God's."[289] This is a temple of the Holy Spirit, not an instrument for eating,

---

288 1 Cor 6:19
289 1 Cor 6:20

drinking, pleasure, and such. One might say that this body is just some dirt. An artist can tell you that the body is a work of art: "I could sit before a body and draw pictures or carve sculptures"—the artist sees the body as a work of art. What is your perception of the body? According to your valuation of the body, you will live your life.

Valuing Spiritual Power

What is your valuation of the spirit? Does your spirit take the same valuation as your body? If your spirit is ill, do you seek out all the spiritually trained specialists to see what to do about your spirit? Or are you oblivious to it if it falls ill? Whereas, if you feel that your body is just a little sick you go and seek checkups, x-rays, and tests. On the other hand, if your spirit is sick, do you even notice? Sometimes you are oblivious—this is if you are a person who does not care about the spirit, but if you care about your spirit you will watch over your spirit. You will give it spiritual food, spiritual medicine, spiritual health, spiritual training, and will care more for your spirit than you care about your body. A person's valuations of the spirit and of the body are what determine the personality.

Valuing Human Beings

Take another example, what is your valuation of human beings? Do you consider every person you meet as your brother or sister? Or do you have specific brethren, and the others are not, but rather rivals, enemies, a different denomination, call it what you will? Do you respect each person's humanity? If a person is valuable, you will respect that person's humanity. If you respect each person's humanity, you will love each person; you will not harm anyone, will not wrong anyone, will not hurt anyone, and will not disgrace anyone, because each person will be valuable in your eyes. For some people, humans have no value. It makes no difference to them if a person is saddened or not. If you ask them if they upset this person, they would ask, "Who is this person anyway!" You might respond: "Who is this person? He is a human being!" They might reply: "What do you mean a human being? This person is valueless!" People who speak for people's rights consider a person something else: a brother to you, an image of you. If you value a person you will be concerned for each person's life, health, feelings, and comfort. You would be unable to offend a person or be a stumbling block, because you would say, "God will require this person's blood from me on the last day." You would not consent to wrong anyone, and you would not accept for a person to spend one night upset with you. There is one who sees each person as a son of God, saying, "Will I offend one of God's children? That is impossible"; the image of God, "Will I offend one in God's image"; the creation of God, "Will I offend one of God's creations?"

Valuing the Human Soul

If you knew the value of the human soul, you would appreciate the value of service—the value of saving one soul. The Lord, out of His valuation of the one soul, and His respect for the one soul, once walked six hours for the sake of the Samaritan woman. He gave us an example of how one leaves the 99 to seek the one lost soul. This one soul is valuable to God, unlike people who enter a war and a bomb kills some thousands, and it makes no difference; canons kills some thousands, and it make no difference; a war in which some thousands die, and it does not matter. What is the value of this human soul? What is the value of the soul? Our Lord, for the sake of any soul, is willing to send angels, prophets, apostles, teachers, preachers, priests, and shepherds for one human soul. Our Lord might personally appear to a person. Each time He appears to a person and speaks, this is the value of the human soul. Redemption reveals to us the value of the human soul to God. What is the value of the human soul? Could you imagine that for God the value of the human soul reached the point of incarnation and redemption! And to others this soul has no value: "What is this soul?" A person's valuation for all matters makes up their personality, actions, and behaviors, not only in treating others, but also in treating God.

Valuing Prayer

Take your valuation of prayer, for example; what is your valuation of prayer? Is it the key to heaven, to which you resort when you are cornered? Is prayer to you the open door in hard times so that in hardships you resort to prayer? Is prayer to you a duty you have to fulfill, even if you force or compel yourself, while not wanting to do it—to you it is a canon, a canon you have to complete—is this what prayer is to you? Is prayer to you an order and a divine commandment, or is prayer to you spiritual food with which your spirit is fed? Is prayer to you spiritual pleasure? Is prayer to you true life? Is prayer to you the connection between you and God? According to your valuation of prayer you will either pray or not pray. If your prayers are simply a chore, then you quickly end them, and once they are finished you say, "Thank God"; not "Thank You God for allowing me to speak with You", but, "Thank God I'm finished with the words. I could pursue my other pleasures now, and, thank God that it's over." But, if to you prayer is a pleasure you would not want it to end; when you come to end a prayer you would try to prolong it, and say, "Oh, how I love Your name! It is my meditation all the day ... I will lift up my hands in Your name. My soul shall be satisfied as with marrow and fatness."[290] What exactly is prayer to you? What is your valuation of prayer? Is it one of the commandments, or one of your pleasures?

---

290 Cf. Ps 119:97; 63:4-5

Valuing the Commandment

The same applies to fasting, and to every other commandment. Concerning the commandments, what is your valuation of them? Is it simply a verse in the Bible or divine orders? Is it what would bring you to Hades if you do not obey? What is a commandment? Are commandments a light which illumines the way: "Your word is a lamp to my feet and a light to my path"?[291] Are commandments something you are forced to do because it is a divine order required of you? And therefore, you have to force yourself to fulfill the commandment, and had you not forced yourself you would never have fulfilled it? Does fulfilling commandments bring joy to you? God drew out the way for you to reach the Kingdom, so do you feel that fulfilling the commandments is the path leading to the Kingdom? If you know this, you will love the commandments and say with St. John the apostle, "His commandments are not burdensome,"[292] and hence fulfilling the commandments will not be a burden to you. What is your valuation of fulfilling God's commandments?

Valuing Sin

Let us take sin for example; what is your valuation of sin? One person values sin as one of the pleasures, and therefore finds difficulty abandoning sin. To one who takes pleasure in smoking, drinking, adultery, or eating and drinking excessively (eating and drinking is not a sin, but gluttony is), sin is a pleasure. Like one who gambles and finds pleasure in gambling, to the point of selling his or her house's furniture in order to play. For this person sin is a pleasure, therefore it is a struggle to abandon sin. Abandoning sin requires great labor, because sin is a pleasure. The most difficult thing is for sin to become a person's pleasure. Is sin to you a kind of human weakness, you might say, "I don't like sin, but I'm weak?" Is sin to you *compulsory*—like one who needs a vacation, and

291 Ps 119:105
292 1 Jn 5:3

lies to take sick leave, and the doctor also lies, but one feels *compelled* saying, "We are making things easier this way"? Or one who finds that bribery is *obligatory*, to move things along, claiming, "This is against my will"—some sins we consider to be *obligatory sins*. For example lying, one will tell you "It is *obligatory*. Will I tell the truth and suffer the consequences? I had to lie. It was something *obligatory*." What is sin to you? Is sin to you something necessary, like one who says, "I have to get angry and defend my dignity," not considering it a sin: "Is this also a sin, that a person stands up for dignity!" What is sin to you?

Valuing the Concept of Sin

Do you look at sin with a simple glance, or is it mutiny and rebellion against God? Is sin to you separation from God? Is sin to you defilement? Is sin to you death? Sin is death: "Be dead indeed to sin."[293] What is sin to you? According to your valuation of sin, you will be able to determine if you will be able to abandon or remain in it. The one who values sin lightly, saying, "Don't be nitpicky. Don't make a fuss. Why make everything so difficult? Let us live a little," this one could never abandon sin. How can this one abandon it? To him, it is an obsession. Another person sees sin as a shame, "How then can I do this great wickedness, and sin against God?"[294] It is impossible! This one is unable to approve of sin, because sin does not agree with the status as a child of God, the image and likeness of God. What is our valuation of sin? Do we have the kind of conscience that could swallow a camel and finds an excuse and justification for every sin? Or do we have the good conscience that looks at matters in the right way? What is sin to you? If it is easy you will fall into it, if it is difficult you will ask, "How then can I do this great wickedness, and sin against God?" Let us reexamine our valuation of matters—reevaluate the way we measure things; all our understanding and judgments on all matters—and

---

293 Rom 6:11
294 Gen 39:9

stand before God with a good conscience: "The wise man's eyes are in his head, but the fool walks in darkness."[295] The intelligent person could understand everything and know the value of everything, evaluating matters, their results, their effects on eternity, and on this life on earth.

Glory be to God forever. Amen.

---

295 Eccl 2:14

HIS HOLINESS POPE SHENOUDA III
ANSWERS THE QUESTIONS OF MONASTICS

I

In the Name of the Father, the Son, and the Holy Spirit, One God. Amen.

Q: What is the meaning of spiritual fatherhood?

Spiritual fatherhood leads a person in the life of the spirit. It is the fatherhood of the confession father and/or of the spiritual guide, or it is one person if the confession father is the spiritual guide. Spiritual fatherhood is often found in the Holy Bible, including St. Paul's words in speaking of Timothy as his "beloved and faithful son ... a true son in the faith,"[296] or when he speaks of Titus as "a true son,"[297] or in his letter to Philemon regarding Onesimus whom he describes as "my son Onesimus, whom I have begotten while in my chains."[298] Also, in speaking of all those who received the faith at his hands, he says, "My little children, for whom I labor in birth."[299] St. Paul speaks much of this spiritual fatherhood. Also, St. John the apostle writes: "My little children, these things I write to you, so that you may not sin."[300] Spiritual fatherhood was also present in the Old Testament, as Elisha spoke of Elijah as, "My father, my father, the chariot of Israel and its horsemen!"[301] Spiritual fatherhood is mentioned abundantly in the Bible. In the monastic life, spiritual fatherhood is parenthood that leads a person in the spiritual life, leading to our Lord, and

296 1 Cor 4:17; 1 Tim 1:2
297 Titus 1:4
298 Philem 1:10
299 Gal 4:19
300 1 Jn 2:1
301 2 Kg 2:12

directing the person on the upright spiritual path.

Q: What are the obligations of the spiritual father to his son and what are the obligations of the son to the father?

We will stick to the obligations of the son to the father, so that you might not begin analyzing the obligations of the fathers. God will judge you for your obligations as sons, so we will stick to your own obligations. He will not judge you for what the fathers do. Each father performs his role according to his situation; not all people are the same.

Spiritual fatherhood is a burden. I have tried it, and it is not an easy burden. I lived the solitary life when I was a monk, but this issue of spiritual fatherhood was put on me since monks confessed to me, and it placed all the monastery politics inside my head, to the point that I considered withdrawing. Each monk has his own responsibilities, and if each one comes to complain of his duties and his relationships with others, after ten or twelve come by, the confession father will certainly have all the monastery's problems in his head. It is not an easy task.

The difficulty of the fatherhood also depends on the extent of obedience of the sons. One father might give advice, but the son is unable to follow it, or does not want to follow through. We are now addressing the issue of the obedience of the sons, as the Holy Bible says: "Obey those who rule over you, [the Arabic text reads "Obey those who guide you"] and be submissive, for they watch out for your souls, as those who must give account. Let them do so with joy and not with grief, for that would be unprofitable for you."[302] There are two points here: 1) they will give an account of you, and 2) that they are not grieved. Do not let your spiritual father grieve over you and your disobedience. When you submit to spiritual guidance, the father rejoices over your success. However, when he finds that you are inattentive, defiant, or disobedient then this word, "grief," applies.

Another issue that troubles the confession father is a son

---

302 Heb 13:17

who already has his mind set and comes to the confession father only to take consent; if consent is not granted then a debate ensues. The true spiritual son takes the words of his spiritual father with faith, without disputing; in contrast to one who is self-directing (only seeking the lawful permission to follow through with his plans), otherwise he becomes upset. Another type refrains from asking the confession father regarding issues to which the confession father would not agree, but only discusses the issues to which he knows the confession father would agree, and then asks, "Did I disobey you in anything?" "It is true that you did not disobey me, but simultaneously, you followed your own will." The correct monastic life is for a person not to follow his own will, but to have faith in the confession father and in his directions. If you do not have this faith, then there is a lack of trust to behave as a son. Likewise, with this lack of trust, you do not share anything that would allow you to benefit from the guidance of your confession and/or spiritual father; you are following your own will.

Q: How could practicing discipleship and the sacrament of confession in the monasteries return to the power and wisdom that used to be in the lives of the early fathers?

The first point for you in confession is that you confess to our Lord personally, and then you confess to our Lord in the hearing of the priest. Confession in the church is the sacrament of repentance. You should repent, confess your sins to God, and then go confess your sins to God in the hearing of the priest; then the remission will come to you from God on the mouth of the priest. You cannot separate God from the sacrament of confession and repentance.

How can you undergo the sacrament of confession? First, you need to repent. Most people come to confess without repenting. This shows in the fact that they continually relapse to that sin. One who repents does not repeat the sin; one who repents is freed from this sin. Therefore, for our saintly fathers, and the penitent saints such as St. Moses [the Strong],

St. Augustine, St. Pelagia, St. Mary of Egypt and the like, repentance was a turning point in their lives. They did not return to those sins again. It was more than a turning point; it was a point of growth in the life of holiness.

If you want to be at the level of the early fathers, what prevents you from repentance? Regardless of the circumstances in the monastery, what prevents you from repenting? What prevents you from pouring out yourself before God and telling Him, "Against You, You only, have I sinned, and done this evil in Your sight"?[303] This is repentance and confession. Next you come to confess before the priest; while you are confessing to him, you must feel that you are confessing to God in the hearing of the priest, and taking the absolution from God on the mouth of the priest. There is nothing to prevent you from repenting and confessing, regardless of the condition of the monastery. Look at the anchorites who spent sixty years without seeing a human face. How do you think they lived? Nothing prevents a person from repenting and living with God regardless of the circumstances.

Q: Christianity retained certain Jewish rituals and abandoned others. Please clarify why Christianity left the bloody sacrifice, but kept the custom of the incense.

Christianity abandoned the bloody sacrifice because Christ replaced it; He is the New Testament Sacrifice that replaced the bloody sacrifices: "For indeed Christ, our Passover, was sacrificed for us. Therefore let us keep the feast, not with old leaven, nor with the leaven of malice and wickedness, but with the unleavened bread of sincerity and truth."[304] Our Lord Jesus Christ took the place of the Passover lamb. Likewise regarding the other sacrifices; in the New Testament, Christ is the whole burnt offering, the trespass offering, the sin offering, the Passover, etc. And so, the sacrifice continues, as our Lord "did not come to destroy but to fulfill."[305] The bloody sacrifice prefigured Christ, and so when the One

303 Ps 51:4
304 1 Cor 5:7–8
305 Mt 5:17

prefigured came, the symbol was removed.

Christianity kept the rite of the incense because the incense was not symbolic of a future event. The sacrifice was a symbol, but the incense is not a symbol; it is prayer in itself, and so it remains. Incense is present in Chapters 5 and 8 of the Book of The Revelation.

Q: What is the meaning of what is said in the Divine Liturgy of St. Gregory: "established the rising of the choir of the incorporeal among men"?[306]

The incorporeal beings are the angels. He established the presence of the angels standing with the humans. The church is not simply a solo group of humans; it is also made up of a group of angels who are surrounding this group of humans. In every church, there are angels. Whenever we pray, we say, "Hail to the church, the house of the angels."[307] There are angels of the sanctuary and of the altar. The last verse in the first chapter of the Letter to the Hebrews describes angels as "all ministering spirits sent forth to minister for those who will inherit salvation";[308] therefore, there are many angels who exist for the sake of those who are set for salvation. They encourage them, help them, pray for them, intercede for them, etc.

There are also angels who surround us: "The angel of the Lord encamps all around those who fear Him, and delivers them."[309] Jacob the patriarch spoke of "the Angel who has redeemed me from all evil."[310] There are angels (messengers) for annunciations. There are also guardian angels. Angels are around humans continually. We are not alone. These are the choir of the incorporeal among men. The history of angels is frequently mentioned in the Old and New Testaments. Angels are very present in our lives. There are also angels who receive the souls of the just, as was said of poor Lazarus

306 (H and H 2007), 267.
307 (The Holy Psalmody 1990), 243. This is taken from the Morning Doxology.
308 Heb 1:14
309 Ps 34:7
310 Gen 48:16

who "was carried by the angels to Abraham's bosom."[311] Recall the miracles of Archangel Michael; we also continually build churches in his name. We hold feasts for the angels; we celebrate Archangel Michael on the twelfth of every Coptic month. We celebrate generally for the angels and their miracles.

---

311 Lk 16:22

HIS HOLINESS POPE SHENOUDA III
ANSWERS THE QUESTIONS OF MONASTICS

II

In the Name of the Father, the Son, and the Holy Spirit, One God. Amen.

Q: How can a monastic practice solitude and stillness inside the monastery?

Practicing solitude and stillness comes gradually; once one dresses in the monastic habit, one does not instantly experience solitude and stillness. While interacting in the community, you need to realize your internal flaws and treat them first so that when you do shut yourself in solitude and stillness, you shut in a healthy, flawless self. Otherwise, you might shut yourself in the cell and likewise shut in your mistakes. As St. Isaac the Syrian said, "Such a person spends a hundred years in his cell, and does not even learn how one should sit."[312] In the community, one tries to attain the community virtues before attaining the virtues of solitude. Some such virtues that you gain in the monastic community are tolerance, placidity, forgiveness, stillness, and voluntary silence. Where could you find offenses in solitude in order to practice these virtues? In solitude, there is no one with whom to talk, and so you live in involuntary silence, but in the community, there are the guarding of the senses and the guarding of the tongue. Guarding the senses is a virtue found in the community because in the desert there is nothing for the senses to gather. Likewise with guarding the tongue, you must gain the virtue of silence in the community before you venture out to solitude. Some people are simply unable to

---

312 (Hausherr 1990), 72.

keep silent. If they are quiet for one half of an hour, they become disturbed, as they need any reason to talk, and so they seek any passerby with whom they can chat. They are incapable of keeping to themselves. The Holy Bible says, "My brethren, let not many of you become teachers, knowing that we shall receive a stricter judgment. For we all stumble in many things."[313] How could this type of person live in solitude? If this person entered solitude, this one would seek to leave it, looking for someone to guide. A story by John Cassian comes to mind:

> I remember an elder, when I was staying in the desert of Scete, who went to the cell of a certain brother to pay him a visit, and when he had reached the door heard him muttering inside, and stood still for a little while, wanting to know what it was that he was reading from the Bible or repeating by heart (as is customary) while he was at work. And when this most excellent eavesdropper diligently applied his ear and listened with some curiosity, he found that the man was induced by an attack of this spirit to fancy that he was delivering a stirring sermon to the people. And when the elder, as he stood still, heard him finish his discourse and return again to his office, and give out the dismissal of the catechumens, as the deacon does, then at last he knocked at the door, and the man came out, and met the elder with the customary reverence, and brought him in and (for his knowledge of what had been his thoughts made him uneasy) asked him when he had arrived, for fear lest he might have taken some harm from standing too long at the door: and the old man joking pleasantly replied, "I only got here while you were giving out the dismissal of the catechumens."[314]

Here, the brother imagined that he was giving an oration. This is one of the wars that strike monastics—the honor of lecturing seculars and guiding them. This type of person should not live in solitude. Among the community virtues that a person should gain are the virtues of silence, distancing from seculars, and distancing from guiding. If you have a longing to guide others, then it is impossible for you to live

---

313 Jas 3:1–2
314 (Library 1998), NPNF Series 2, Vol 11, 570–571.

in solitude.

The first step a person takes toward a life of solitude is gaining the virtues of the community. Next, one lives in the community and tries to discover the faults in order to correct them. One time, a monk went to the abbot of the monastery asking to be released to go to another monastery. The abbot asked if anyone troubled him, and he responded, "No, all the monks are saints, but I need to go attain virtues. Here no one wrongs me, that I may forgive him; no one offends me, that I may pardon him; no one persecutes me, that I may endure him, so, where will I attain these virtues? I need to go somewhere to attain virtues."[315] The abbot blessed him and released him, because he saw that he was a laboring monk. Certainly, he dismissed him to a difficult monastery in which he might attain these virtues. This story and other similar stories can be found in the book I published for you on *Anger*.

As I previously stated, it is first necessary for one to gain the virtues of the community before pursuing a life of solitude. These include silence, avoiding teaching, having good relations with others, gaining people's love, and as St. Anthony said, "making everyone bless you."[316] This means receiving each person's blessings and their prayers for you. This is the best advice we could give you in the community life.

Among the community virtues is promptness to the church and her services, especially the Vespers, Midnight, and the Prime bells. It is necessary to attain this virtue so that these services do not become routine prayers, such that you find yourself rushing through them until the Divine Liturgy is over, and you leave the church without having gained anything. Gain the spirituality of prayer and learn how to pray. Also among the virtues of the community is the need to grow accustomed to praying. Some people can barely finish the psalms and are unable to pray any further. Your success in prayer is gauged by the following: When it is time to finish prayer, do you long to continue praying, with no desire to finish, not wanting to end your standing in the

---

315 (Beni-Suef Publication Committee 1977), 324.

316 Saint Anthony, cf. (Budge, Paradise 1984) II, 8 {19}; (Beni-Suef Publication Committee 1977), 198.

presence of God? Do you pray with spirituality, emotion, love, faith, reverence, fervor, meditation, and understanding? The more one increases in prayer and meditation, the more one enters into solitude (in order to continue this prayer that is unattainable in the community), and the further one enters into silence—not the negative silence, but the positive kind. Negative silence is refraining from speaking, while positive silence is giving an opportunity for prayer and meditation. Our saintly fathers practiced silence, not only as a means of avoiding sins of the tongue, but also in order to give an opportunity for meditation and prayer. When you reach this point, then you may enter the life of solitude.

The fathers set solitude as gradual steps. First is solitude during the day while one worked in the community. One finished the day's work and then entered solitude. St. Isaac[317] says that the second step is silence of weeks—during the week, one is shut in; and at the end of the week, one exits to meet the fathers, attend the Divine Liturgy, partake of the Holy Eucharist, receive the blessings of the fathers, perhaps ask some questions of the elders, and then return to solitude. The next step is silence for several weeks, like one who locks himself in during the Virgin Mary's Fast, the Holy Great Fast, all the fasting days, and finally venturing into the life of solitude and retreat in the desert and wilderness. All of this occurs under spiritual guidance, lest one strays along the way.

Q: Is it sufficient for a monastic to live as if living in the world, in order to fulfill the vow of voluntary poverty, even if one is unable to live on scant food, or without medicines, books, and other equipment? Also, the story of Fr. Anastasi, who lived in the tomb for a long time, pricks the conscience.

Certainly, read the story of Fr. Anastasi. I wrote it, and it had an impact on me. It provides an image of the practical meaning of dying to the world. St. Paul spoke of "those who

---

317 (Miller 1984), 377, 379.

use this world as not misusing it."[318] You could live as if you are not using the world, taking from it only what is necessary and leaving the rest. Set before you are a variety of foods; you could take what you want and refrain from what you do not want. No one forces you to take the most delectable foods, and no one forces you to consume more of certain types.

Do likewise with everything else. Do you have time? You might say, "I do not have time during work," but you have time at night, as St. Isaac says, "The night is set apart to engage in prayer."[319] We say in the Psalm, "Behold, bless the Lord, all you servants of the Lord, who by night stand in the house of the Lord! Lift up your hands in the sanctuary, and bless the Lord."[320] The night is full of calmness, stillness, and silence; you are able to sit alone with our Lord at night. Believe me, those who are able to befriend the night are able to live spiritually during the day. When you win the friendship of the night, you fill the night with prayers, weeping, tears, and praises. This time that you spend with God at night will follow you during the day and leave its influence in your mind, heart, character, and interactions.

Likewise with the Psalms, they especially give us an idea of how life should be, from every angle. They are not all simply prayers; they have an educational aspect. For example, the following passages are educational: "Blessed is the man who walks not in the counsel of the ungodly, nor stands in the path of sinners, nor sits in the seat of the scornful; but his delight is in the law of the Lord, and in His law he meditates day and night";[321] take this part from the epistle of St. Paul to the Ephesians in the Prime prayer: "I, therefore, the prisoner of the Lord, beseech you to walk worthy of the calling with which you were called, with all lowliness and gentleness, with longsuffering, bearing with one another in love";[322] likewise, these verses from the Prime prayer: "Lord, who may abide in Your tabernacle? Who may dwell in Your holy hill? He who walks uprightly, and works righteousness, and speaks the truth

---

318 1 Cor 7:31
319 Cf. (Miller 1984), 308, 370–372.
320 Ps 134:1
321 Ps 1:1–2
322 Eph 4:1–2

in his heart";[323] note also the Holy Gospel of the Sixth Hour, the Beatitudes, which are part of the Sermon on the Mount. One who prays much also receives beneficial life education.

If you are unable to find calmness during the day, borrow from the calmness of the night, and from it you will have leftover credit for the day. The words of the prayers will remain in your mind and in your heart. This applies to the one who seeks; the one who does not seek blames the environment, the duties, and the visitors. It is better to blame yourself because you did not borrow from the friendship of the night: "Behold, bless the Lord, all you servants of the Lord, who by night stand in the house of the Lord! Lift up your hands in the sanctuary, and bless the Lord."[324] David the Prophet was very busy during the day with the kingdom, the army, the family, the problems, and many things, but he said, "I remember You on my bed, I meditate on You in the night watches ... At daybreak You hear my voice ... At midnight I will rise to give thanks to You."[325] He said all these psalms during the night, and so during his nightly prayers, he regained what he had lost during his preoccupations during the day.

You have a long way to go!

We are still in the stage of trials and struggle, and will continue to fight and struggle until we depart from this body. St. Paul says, "You have not yet resisted to bloodshed, striving against sin."[326] Oh, that we would memorize this verse! Not only should we not commit a sin mentioned in the Ten Commandments, rather, even our feeling that we have attained, is a sin. We have a long way to go. If you see the way saints pray, the way they speak of their sins, you will be amazed. Have we reached the glorious liberty of the children of God? If you say that you have, the devil will say, "Come! I will try you! I will test your freedom! Is it rock solid freedom or not!" We have a long way to go.

323 Ps 15:1–2
324 Ps 134:1
325 Ps 63:6; 119:62; (Wansbrough 1985) NJB 5:3.
326 Heb 12:4

I remember, long ago, I had in my cell a small table close to the ground where I would write while seated. I placed on this table a paper which read: "You still have a long way to go." Whenever I came to work, write, or eat, I would read this paper. Believe me my brethren, one time I was reading the book of St. John Climacus—this book has thirty steps—and as I read the first step, I thought, "Where is this? I have not even reached this first step yet, what about the rest of the thirty steps!" Will you read this book and say, "I have reached the glorious liberty of the children of God?" Read the step on death to the world and see if you have reached it. Read the step on renunciation and see if you have reached it. Read the step on penitence and see if you have reached it. You have a long way to go. Joyous is the person who resounds daily with St. Arsenius the Great, who, despite all his virtues, said to the Lord, "I have done nothing good in your sight, but according to your goodness, let me now make a beginning of good."[327] They found Abba Sisoes struggling at the time of his departure: they said to him, "What do you see, abba?" He said to them, "I see beings coming towards me, and I am begging them to leave me a little while so that I may repent." One of the old men said to him, "And even if they allow you a respite, can you now profit by it and do penance?" The old man said to him, "If I am not able to do that, at least I can groan a little over my soul and that is enough for me."[328]

You have a long way to go. Beware of such thoughts.

Young Saints?

There are people who reached a high level of spirituality while they were still youth. We see St. Moses [the Strong] greeting Zachariah and asking him for a beneficial word (a similar incident occurred with St. Macarius[329]) and this youth responds with astonishment: "Are you, Father, the light and

327 (Ward, Sayings 1984), 9 {3}.
328 Ibid., 221 {49}.
329 See (Vivian, Saint Macarius the Spiritbearer: Coptic Texts Relating to Saint Macarius the Great 2004), 124–125.

pillar of the wilderness, asking me?" St. Moses answered, "I know, by the Holy Spirit, that you have words from which I could benefit."[330]

There are other examples of youth who have reached very high levels of spirituality. Take, for example, Theodore, the disciple of Pachomius, who guided many people and established many monasteries during his father Pachomius' lifetime while he was still a youth. Likewise, St. John the Short was at this same stature of amazing maturity while he was still young, to the point that it was said that he had "all Scetis hanging from his little finger."[331] Another example of a youth who reached a very high level of monasticism, and an amazing personality of whom I speak frequently, is St. Misail the Anchorite. He came to the monastery while still young, perhaps when he was twelve years old. He amazed Abba Isaac, the abbot of the monastery; when Misail arrived to the monastery he distinctively greeted Abba Isaac, who was sitting among the monks, as a father. When Abba Isaac asked him, "How did you know me?" He answered him, "I saw in your face the spirit of the abbot." Misail entered isolation when he was about fourteen and became an anchorite when he was seventeen years old.[332] This is an extraordinary person; not all people are this way. When we speak of some youth who were on a very high level of monasticism, of mentality, of discernment, and of wisdom, we do not mean all people. Our Lord chose the child Samuel to direct a message to Eli, the high priest. Will every child be this way? No, each one differs.

Q: How can a monastic progress in the life of solitude inside the monastery?

The fathers said first to begin with the community virtues before venturing into solitude. What does it mean to begin with the community virtues? For example, the virtues you could undertake among people are, endurance, placidity,

330 Cf. (Ward, Sayings 1984), 68 {3}.
331 Ibid., 93 {36}.
332 (El-Soriany 1993), 165–172.

silence, calmness, forgiveness, and toil out of love for the brethren. If you spring into solitude without community virtues, then you are storing the sins inside you and only taking on the image of solitude. This is like the story of the monk who had the sin of anger remaining in him:

A certain brother while he was in the community was restless and frequently moved to wrath. And he said within himself, "I shall go and live in some place in solitude: and when I have no one to speak to or to hear, I shall be at peace and this passion of anger will be stilled." So he went forth and lived by himself in a cave. One day he filled a jug for himself with water and set it on the ground, but it happened that it suddenly overturned. He filled it a second time, and again it overturned. And he filled it a third time and set it down, and it overturned again. And in a rage he caught up the jug and broke it.[333]

Anger was stored inside him. Even in the cave, if you cannot find someone with whom to be angry, you will be upset by the weather, by the insects, or by any matter. The more you gain the community virtues, the more you attain purity of heart. If you reach purity of heart, then you will be able to worship God in solitude with a pure heart. One, who had not reached the step of gaining community virtues, went to the abbot asking to venture into solitude. The abbot asked the reason, and the monk explained that he was troubled by the actions of the brethren in the community. The abbot responded, "If you are unable to endure the troubles of the brethren in the community, how will you endure the troubles of the devils in solitude?"[334] You must first attain the community virtues. In solitude, who will you find, with whom to be angry or to forgive? None, no one is there to harm you.

Second, you have to grow in the life of prayer. If you cannot spend much time praying, you will be bored when you venture into solitude. How will you pass the time? Grow in the life of meditation, in spiritual thought, and in spiritual reading, so that you may use your time wisely.

Also, you need to grow in humility, because in solitude

---

333 Unknown Elder, (Thornton and S 1998), 94–95 {xxxiii}; cf. (Ward, Desert Fathers 2003), 71 {33}.
334 Cf. (Chryssavgis 2003), 70.

you will gain the title of "the Solitary." If you are not humble, this title will trouble you: it will bring you vainglory, boasting, and praise from people. You have to grow in the life of humility in order to endure solitude. When you sit in solitude, people will say, "We want to go to this solitary to receive a beneficial word." You will find yourself becoming a source of beneficial words flowing out of your mouth, which will bring wars upon you. If you are not humble, then you will lose all that you have.

HIS HOLINESS POPE SHENOUDA III
ANSWERS THE QUESTIONS OF MONASTICS

III

In the Name of the Father, the Son, and the Holy Spirit, One God. Amen.

Q: What is death to the world in monasticism?

Monasticism begins first in the heart. It enters the monastic rite during ordination to take on the monastic image, and then it extends to the actual life. This is monasticism. You take on the monastic image because you are already monastic internally (the heart inside has already died to the world). Do you think that we put the novices to death during the monasticism rite? If the world is not dead within them, then our prayer simply gives them the image, the monastic garb, the cowl, the girdle, the new name; but monasticism, in essence, is death to the world. It is internal death, inside the heart. On the day of ordination, the Church sanctions this death, and gives the monastic a new name (the old name having died). Yet, is it a true death, or is every monastic looking internally and saying, "Lazarus, come forth!"[335] beckoning to the old self to come out again? If a person has died, then that one has died; if you want to live the life of the dead, then enter monasticism.

This is best expressed in a story I wrote long ago titled *Fr. Anastasi*. Please read it. I remember that I narrated this story to an engineer, Sameh (currently Bishop Samuel of Shebeen-El-Kanater). I had told the story, and so they asked me to record it. This was the first time in my life that I saw a recorder; I did not know what a recorder was or how it works.

---

335 Jn 11:43

When I published the Keraza Magazine in 1965, I placed this story in the first issue and under it was my signature, then I republished it in the Keraza in the early '90s.

I will give you a simple idea of it, so you will know the importance of this story. It begins: Fr. Anastasi was greatly surprised as he awoke feeling a veil on his face. He lifted his hand to remove it, and a cross fell from his hand. What was this veil, and what was this cross? Also, what was this darkness? He remembered that he had left his window open, and the moonlight was beaming in. Also, what was this awful stench? It resembled the scent of death. He was disturbed and, wanting to check, he looked here and there, and finding dead corpses he knew that he was in the monastery catacombs. Had he really died and been buried, or had they assumed him dead and buried him, or had he died and risen? He did not know. All he knew was that he was dead in the eyes of the monastery and of the world. If he were to go out to the people, they might suffer shock; therefore, he must live as one that has died.

How, as a dead person, did he cope with regards to his food, his drink, his actions, etc.? In the middle of the night, in the dark, he would go out and take a loaf of bread, some leftover food from unwashed dishes, or some vegetables from the monastery garden, and return to lock himself in as dead. As a dead person, he would not speak to people. As a dead person, he would not respond when he was accused. Once, some monks were sitting outside the tomb talking, and one praised him while the other criticized him, but he answered neither of them. As a dead person, he did not receive letters from people, nor did he write to anyone. Another thing: long ago, he used to read spiritual and religious books, and the abundance of reading did not give him an opportunity to meditate; but now, he began to ruminate on what he had read long ago, and began to meditate. He had no books, so he began to pray and train on prayer. As a dead person, positions would be vacated in the church, but he would not feel it, nor would anyone nominate him. He neither considered positions, nor did people consider him. The story continues in this fashion.

He read very little; if he greatly longed to read, then at

midnight or shortly thereafter, when he sensed that no one was around, he went to the church, opened the book, read a couple of words, and took his leave. One time, while he was leaving, someone saw him, and thinking he was an anchorite, asked for his blessing. He blessed him (unable to debate with him) and they both fled. He returned to his grave and refused to leave for a few days because people started to wonder when the anchorites would come.

Read the story. It will show you what death to the world means. It says that long ago, during his first life, his cell was full of many objects: the desk, the pens, the papers, the books, the utensils, his closet full of clothes, the chairs, a bed, etc. Now he had nothing. Now he did not even have a cell, and did not even own the tomb in which he was laid. From time to time they would inter in another corpse, and he would hold his breath and rush to cover himself with the veil and the cross, as if he were not there, until they left, and then he could *enjoy* the new scent. He began to regret all the objects he used to have in his cell; he would just simply look at the kitchen with its dishes, plates, mugs, utensils, forks. Now he had nothing. He used nothing. Ultimately, try to read the story.

As I was saying, I recorded this story before becoming a bishop (1962), perhaps in 1961, for Sameh, who was in Fagallah, along with a youth who became a monk thereafter, and asked to take on the name of Anastasi. Whoever wants to live a monastic life needs to live as Fr. Anastasi did in the tomb; see how he lived. Will someone say, "No you have to break your monastic principles?" No. No one will forbid anyone who wants to walk on the right path. Furthermore, if there are difficulties and you overcome them, then your reward will be much greater.

Q: Could you give clear examples of applying "the unity

of the spirit,"[336] and practical steps to the unity of the spirit?

"All who believed were of one spirit, with one mind, and had all things in common"[337]—this is unity of spirit. There are many ways to attain one mind. One example is, during mealtime, while they silently listened, the fathers read *The Paradise of the Fathers* (or any other similar ascetic or spiritual book), perhaps the teachings of Abba Isaiah the Solitary, St. Barsanuphius, St. John of Lycopolis, Mar Evagrius, or the like. All these give one mindset, to attain to the unity of the spirit. You cannot attain unity of spirit without unity of mind.

Unity of spiritual direction could also lead here, but if each person is moving in a different direction, then how will it lead to unity? St. Paul says, "One Lord, one faith, one baptism."[338] Likewise, unity of spirit is unity of faith, but faith is not simply the Creed we recite. Faith branches out into many areas in order for people to attain unity of spirit.

Also, to attain unity of spirit, you need to solve your problems promptly: "Endeavoring to keep the unity of the Spirit in the bond of peace."[339] Do not allow a fellow to be upset with you overnight: "Do not let the sun go down on your wrath."[340] This verse has deeper meanings, but at least do not allow your friend to remain upset with you overnight, but rather, rush instantly to the unity of the spirit. Do not allow the disturbance to remain; rush to resolve it instantly.

Unity of spirit does not prevent variety in monastic method. It is not necessary for people to march on one path. One might move along the solitary path, while another might serve in the monastic community; still, there is unity of spirit.

Regarding the practical steps to unity of spirit, it is best not to gossip about others. Gossiping scatters the unity of spirit. Attempting to reproach others also loses the unity of spirit. Also, guard your tongue if you want to maintain unity of spirit; many people lose unity of spirit as a result of

336 Eph 4:3
337 Acts 2:44; Phil 1:27
338 Eph 4:5
339 Eph 4:3–4
340 Eph 4:26

talking, gossiping, judging, rejoicing over others' failure, or commenting on the actions of others; this is why St. Macarius the Great said, "'Flee, my brothers.' One of the old men asked him, 'Where could we flee to beyond this desert?' He put his finger on his lips and said, 'Flee that.'"[341] If the Holy Bible says, "Do not rejoice when your enemy falls,"[342] then at least do not rejoice when your brother falls. Some people rejoice over others' failures but this is against the unity of spirit. If we have one education and one leadership, if we have one monastic method, if we try to reconcile quickly when there is conflict, if we have common monastic principles, and if we guard our tongues and do not comment on the actions of others or judge others, then in this way, we will approach, as much as is possible, the unity of the spirit.

Unity of spirit may also be attained by praying for each other. In every Divine Liturgy, we pray the Reconciliation Prayer before we lift up the prospherine and begin the Liturgy of the Believers. We also greet each other with a holy kiss; this kiss is meant to be free of "all guile, all hypocrisy, all malice... that we may flee from the likeness of Judas the traitor."[343] If we are being hypocritical toward one another, then it is not a holy kiss, but rather a routine or ritual greeting as the hands greet while the hearts do not. If we had greeted each other with a holy kiss, we would have conserved the unity of the spirit. Sometimes, part of the problem is when the form of worship becomes routine. Each one says to the other, "I have sinned, forgive me ... I have sinned, absolve me," and he is neither forgiving nor absolving, but it is simply a routine with handshakes, the appearance of forgiveness, and empty responses in the Divine Liturgy. If we take worship and monasticism in true spirit, then we will conserve the unity of the spirit.

---

341 (Ward, Sayings 1984), 131.
342 Prov 24:17
343 (H and H 2007), 146, 292 (176, 335 in the 2007 edition).

Q: How can a person reach the point of loving God?

At first, love enters your heart, then you treat each person with love, and then you treat God with this same love. St. John the Beloved says, "He who does not love his brother whom he has seen, how can he love God whom he has not seen?"[344] Try at first to walk in love with all people, on the condition that it is practical love, and not simply emotions or undefined desires. First Corinthians gives us the characteristics of practical love: "Love suffers long and is kind ... does not seek its own ... thinks no evil."[345] Try to reach the point of dealing with all people with love. If love reigns over your heart, then there is nothing in your heart but love. "God is love,"[346] and so God is in your heart.

I published a book on Love. It talks about loving God, loving people, leaving the first Love through spiritual drought, etc. Try to read this book. Generally speaking, to reach the point of loving God, try to talk with God continually. Try to make your conversations with Him emotional. Try harder to solve your problems with God than doing so with people. Try to make all other love exist inside loving God. Each person you love, love as part of your love for God, meaning that you should love others within your love for God, not outside of it; love people with a pure love. When your love for each person is part of your love for God, then you will automatically move to loving God; do not set your virtues apart from God. Our mistake in many situations is that we practice the life of virtue away from God, not as part of our relationship with God.

Q: Please speak to us of God's goodness and love.

Please read my book on Love. The Holy Bible says, "Therefore consider the goodness and severity of God ... toward you, goodness, if you continue in His goodness. Otherwise you

---

344 1 Jn 4:20
345 1 Cor 13:4–5
346 1 Jn 4:8

also will be cut off."[347] Our Lord has both these qualities. Look at the time of His resurrection: when the angel moved the stone "the guards shook for fear of him, and became like dead men,"[348] meanwhile the Marys rejoiced. It is the same incident, but to some it was joyful, while to others it was like death.

This is why, when I published the book entitled *The Fear of God*, I wrote in the introduction that I had desired for a long time to publish this book. From the abundance of talk about God's love, people began to become lax: "God is gentle. Do whatever you want, then say to Him, 'Forgive me,' and He will say, 'You are saved.'" Some people began to abuse God's love as an excuse for disrespect and carelessness. Please try to read much about the fear of God. The Holy Bible says, "The fear of the Lord is the beginning of wisdom."[349] If you walk in the fear of God, you will walk upright, and ultimately reach the love of God.

One cannot come to say, "Perfect love casts out fear!"[350] This is perfect love. Who among us has reached perfect love? The one who has reached perfect love has no fear, but we have not yet reached perfect love.

Q: How could a monastic walk uprightly and not oscillate between two sides, especially when one finds that the life of negligence is taking control?

If the life of negligence is controlling you, then you are not swinging between two ends, you are living in one extreme—negligence. This issue calls for commitment, seriousness, and precision. These three qualities contradict carelessness and vacillating between extremes. If you oscillate between extremes, then you demolish all that you build. Thus, you are continually building and demolishing without stability. One time you sit with God, and another time you leave God and forsake the delight of sitting with Him by walking on a

---

347 Rom 11:22
348 Mt 28:4
349 Prov 9:10
350 1 Jn 4:18

different path. Try to live in the path of precision, seriousness, and commitment. As one person put it, "The kingdom of God wants men"—spiritual masculinity that is! You cannot be wishy-washy; you need to walk with manly seriousness. I am not the one saying this, but rather listen to what David the prophet told his son Solomon: "Be strong, therefore, and prove yourself a man."[351] When a man says a word, he stands by it and does not change it.

You took certain vows before God, but what is your position on these vows? The Psalm says, "Accept, I pray, the freewill offerings of my mouth, O Lord."[352] You took vows. The first vow you took in your life was renouncing the devil at your baptism, it was your vow spoken on your behalf by your mother or father: "I abhor you Satan, with all your impure works, all your evil soldiers, all your wickedness, and all your powers."[353] Are you firm on this vow? The day you became a monastic you vowed to die to the world, you consented to die, and several times they read over you, "and from this soul."[354] In the Thanksgiving Prayer, we pray, "Take them away from us, and from all your people, and from this soul."[355] Thus, you have become simply a soul on which we prayed the prayer of the dead. Are you firm in your vow to die to the world? Death to the world is a very broad subject. Sometimes, a person vows to have died to the world during this prayer, meanwhile this same person is unable to leave a specific duty inside the monastery. You left the whole world; are you unable to leave one duty? This is a vow we take, but perhaps are not serious about. You take a vow every time you take communion; we say, "For each time you eat of this bread and drink of this cup, you proclaim My death, confess My resurrection, and remember Me till I come."[356] Overlooking the part about proclaiming His death and confessing His resurrection (because we do not preach in the monastery), do

---

351 1 Kg 2:2
352 Ps 119:108
353 (Hanna, The Coptic Offices for the Coptic Orthodox Church. Part 1: Bathing, Baptism, Holy Chrism 1995), 69.
354 (H and H 2007), 6.
355 Ibid., 5–6.
356 Ibid., 163.

you remember Him till He comes? There are many vows we take and with which we do not follow through. Each time you repent, each time you confess, you vow to leave the sin and not return to it. Do you abstain from it? Walk seriously. If you vacillate between the sides, you will reach nowhere. What if you walk sometimes on God's path and sometimes on sin's path, and God takes you while you are on sin's path, saying, "This night your soul will be required of you"?[357] What will you do then? Can you guarantee anything?

One time, I found an elderly monk standing long to pray by the relics of the saints. He spoke much, but among his words he said, "Lord, do not take me in a moment of inattention." This is a beautiful saying. When you seesaw between sides, you might be taken in a moment of inattention. You should thank God for not having taken you while you were on the other path. When the angels would have come to take your soul, the demons would have said, "No, this one is ours." This is why, when the Lord Christ approached the time of His death on the cross, He said, "The ruler of this world is coming, and he has nothing in Me."[358] Oh, that you would memorize this verse. When one comes to die and the devil comes to take the soul, one would respond, "You have nothing in me. I have closed out my account with you promptly by repentance, confession, and spiritual growth."

I want to tell you something. Do not be upset by it, but rather remember it: one person comes to the monastery to become a monastic saying, "I will live the life of repentance, and the world has nothing in me," while another comes to become a monastic to begin a new life with new sins—sins suitable for the monastic rite. Of course, there are no sins suitable for monastics, but I mean sins that seculars are unable to do, but monastics can. Did you come to repent, or to commit new sins? Ask yourself this question. Are you praying, "Lord, forgive me my old sins," or are you saying, "And my new sins also, and the sins I adamantly want to commit tomorrow and the day after?"

---

357 Lk 12:20
358 Jn 14:30

Q: Does life before monasticism count?

There was an elderly monk in the monastery, Fr. Paul El-Baramousy as I remember, in the previous generation, who was very old, perhaps over eighty years old. They asked him, "How old are you Fr. Paul?" He answered, "About fifty." They asked him, "Is that possible? Are you really fifty?" He answered them, "My children, the years we spent in the world, before monasticism, do not count." He began counting his age from the time he became a monk.

HIS HOLINESS POPE SHENOUDA III

ANSWERS THE QUESTIONS OF MONASTICS

IV

In the Name of the Father, the Son, and the Holy Spirit, One God. Amen.

Q: How does one reach unceasing prayer? What is the prayer rope, and how can a person train on it?

For a person to reach unceasing prayer, one needs to pray at all times. How can you reach this point? By praying continually. If your mind is continually occupied with prayer, then you will reach unceasing prayer. St. Barsanuphius was asked about unceasing or pure prayer; he gave an amazing response: "It is death to the world."[359] What does this mean? When your heart dies to all that is in the world, then nothing remains in you but connectedness with God, because nothing else occupies you. You do not pray unceasingly because you are preoccupied with other things. You are not free to speak with our Lord because your mind is on other matters. As the Lord Christ said to Martha: "You are worried and troubled about many things. But one thing is needed."[360] As long as you are worried and troubled about many things, it will be impossible for you to reach unceasing prayer. In fact, you will not be able to reach even uninterrupted prayer.

If you are unable to reach unceasing prayer, at least begin with the canonical hours. After you accomplish this, you can enter another practice: praying during work. Next, you can begin to pray while you walk. Then, you will try to pray

---

359 Cf. (Russell 1981), 55.
360 Lk 10:41–42

while you are sitting with people. And finally, you can pray while you are sleeping; this can be done by praying before you sleep until sleep takes over while God's name is on your lips. Through short repeated prayers, one can reach this stage. Repeat a short prayer many times, until it sticks in your memory, and your mind moves in it inadvertently.

Reverence

I will tell you a story. You might consider it an experience, or you might consider it a confession. Consider it what you will, but it occurred to me. When I first began visiting monasteries, I thought of the monastery as an amazing holy land that I longed to see. On my first visit to the monastery, from when I first began to walk from Hukaria, no, from the first time I took permission to visit from Bishop Theophilus (may God repose his soul), I was overjoyed. I took that permission slip in my hand as a Catholic person would clasp onto a remission stamp. When we reached Hukaria, I wondered: "Will I tread on the ground on which treaded St. Arsenius and the three saintly Macarii?" I was ecstatic. When I first saw the monastery, I thought it was an amazing site. I entered the monastery with the utmost reverence; the monastery and the monastery grounds held great reverence within me. With time, my beloved brethren, I grew accustomed to the monastery and what maintained awe and reverence for me was the church. I entered the church in reverence. Then I became a monk, and the church became casual, but what maintained reverence in my sight were the sanctuary and the altar. In time, even these became customary.

Then two things happened to me. One time a group of tourists came to visit the monastery, and I, being the tour guide, entered the church and began to explain. As I found those tourists abandon my explanation and stand before the altar to pray, I said, "'This slap is for your cheek, Arsenius.'[361] Will strangers enter the church in reverence and stand to pray, while you enter to explain?" This was the first slap. After

---

361 (Beni-Suef Publication Committee 1977), 55.

that, once I entered the church, I had to go to the sanctuary, bow before it, enter the sanctuary, and bow before the altar. This is a lesson I took from the tourists. The second slap occurred one day while I was inside the sanctuary. A visitor came and bowed before the sanctuary praying from the depth of his heart in great reverence that revealed itself on his features. I looked at him and said, "This was what I looked like long ago, before I grew accustomed to the sanctuary, the church, and the altar." The more a person grows accustomed to the monastery, the church, the sanctuary, and the altar, the more these things lose their amazing value in the sight of that person. I remember once, a non-Christian Arabian woman came to the monastery requesting some dirt from the sanctuary. She wanted it for the healing of her son. As a woman, she could not enter the monastery or the church, but she had faith; some dust from the sanctuary held great awe, reverence, and dignity in her eyes.

On the feasts of the saints, we blend spices and use them to embalm the box containing the relics of the saints. As a blessing, people crowd to take very small amounts of the spices that touched the box containing the relics of the saints. What they take might not even have touched the box (when we embalm it, only some spices touch the box, while the rest do not). I am cautious on such occasions to blend the spices that touched the box with the rest of the spices. Meanwhile, we have the actual box and the actual relics, and we are indifferent towards them. When we place our hands on the relics, we do so in a routine manner that does not have the magnificent faith of those people. I fear that, with time, we might lose reverence for holy places and holy lands, the monastery, the church, the sanctuary, and the altar.

People who come to visit the monastery cry, "Bless me father, pray for me," because they have not grown accustomed to you. But the workers inside the monastery who have grown accustomed to you and you to them, who see your coming and going, and know your weaknesses and faults, you find that these workers do not greet the monks and priests with the same reverence as those who come from outside of the monastery because they have grown accustomed to

you and to your priesthood. They begin to suddenly feel this
reverence when you pray the Divine Liturgy, because the awe
of the situation, of the traditional prayer, and of the Divine
Mysteries makes them feel the reverence. It is a fierce war
against reverencing the church, the sanctuary, and the altar. I
have reverence for the Sacrament. Thank God, this is the one
thing for which I have not lost awe. This is evident in that we
take every caution with each gem [any particle from the Holy
Body]. This is what remains for us.

Q: Are the Church canons, rites, and theology important for a monastic?

In truth, theology is not so much knowledge or philosophy,
as much as it is a relationship between a person and God. Yet,
I will mention some of the following matters.

In the early ages, monks were the scholars of the Church;
when the theological college halted in Alexandria, it revived
in the monasteries. Before there were printing presses, monks
were the ones who transcribed the holy books. It is reported
that there were about four hundred scribes in the region of
St. Bishoy. They were the ones who transcribed the religious
books, at least the Holy Bible, Old and New Testaments, as
well as the Horologion (the Agpeya) and the ritual books used
in the Church; therefore, they were the most knowledgeable.
One who transcribes is given an opportunity to meditate on
each and every word as it is being transcribed. Therefore, during
the era of Christ, the scribes were the most versed in the law,
regardless of whether or not they obeyed it. An example of
this can be seen when the Magi came asking Herod: "Where
is He who has been born King of the Jews? For we have seen
His star in the east and have come to worship Him.... When
he had gathered all the chief priests and scribes of the people
together, he inquired of them where the Christ was to be
born. So they said to him, 'In Bethlehem of Judea.'"[362] They
were the most well-versed people. This applies to those who
take our Lord's word with depth. In the Church, Scripture is

---

362 Mt 2:2–5

read, and the one who takes these readings with depth could be the most knowledgeable. This is one angle.

From another angle, the Divine Liturgy and ritual books are among the most important sources for understanding theological issues. In the study of theology, when we refer to sources, we say that the primary source is the Holy Bible, the secondary sources are the ritual books, and the tertiary sources are the sayings of the fathers who are considered teachers of the church. One who takes rituals and the ritual books seriously finds treasures placed within the Euchologian,[363] the Horologion, the Psalmody, and the rest of the ritual books. Our ancestors were theological giants in knowledge. All this is from the positive side.

From the negative side, one who does not know theology could be deluded. In our current age, there are some monks who have deviated in theological issues. Also, some monks are simple; they fall into faults without knowing. I remember the first responsibility entrusted to me as a monk was caring for the library in the Syrian Monastery. At first, I coded the books, organized them, and read them as much as I could. In doing this, I would find inside the front cover of a book a curse and an anathema against anyone who removes it from the monastery or contradicts the book; however, the book is full of heresies and innovations. Probably, a person gave it as a gift to a monk, who thanked him for it and prayed for him, without knowing what is written inside this heretical book. Perhaps an unorthodox manuscript, or an incorrect icon, given as a gift, might be placed in the church, meanwhile, it is all wrong.

The monastic studies theological matters, not for educational purposes, but to benefit from them personally. Sometimes when one studies, one seeks to teach others, considering it a buried talent if people do not benefit from this knowledge. If you learn theology for your own personal gain, this is good for you. If you study theology in order to teach others, then you will be fought with venturing outside your rite of isolation and meditation.

---

363 The Divine Liturgy Book.

BIBLIOGRAPHY

Aboseif, Anthony. *Coptic Hymns: A Book of Hymns for all Occasions of the Coptic Year.* Corona: Saint Antonius Coptic Orthodox Church, 2000.

Agpia: The prayer book of the seven canonical hours. Sydney: Coptic Orthodox Publication and Translation, 1997.

Allchin, A M, ed. *Daily Readings with St. Isaac of Syria.* Translated by Sebastian Brock. Springfield: Templegate Publishers, 1990.

Beemen, Bishop. *St. Bishoy.* Malawy: Malawy Antinoe Ashmonin Bishopric, 1981.

Behr, John, ed. *Four Desert Fathers: Pambo, Evagrius, Macarius of Egypt, and Macarius of Alexandria.* Translated by Tim Vivian. Crestwood: St Vladimir's Seminary Press, 2004.

Beni-Suef Publication Committee. *Bustan-El-Ruhban.* 2nd Edition. Beni-Suef: Generation Publishing House, 1977.

—. *Bustan-El-Ruhban.* 2nd Edition. Beni-Suef: Generation Publishing House, 1977.

Bishop Mettaous, HG. *The Sublime Life of Monasticism.* Cairo: Monaliza Press, 2005.

Brakke, David. *Talking Back: A Monastic Handbook for Combating Demons.* Collegeville: Liturgical Press, 2009.

Budge, E A Wallis, trans. *The Paradise of the Holy Fathers.* Revised Edition. II vols. Putty: St. Shenouda Monastery, 2008.

Budge, E A Wallis, trans. *The Paradise of the Holy Fathers.* II vols. Seattle: St Nectarios Press, 1984.

Christ, Christian Education of the National Council of the Churches of, trans. *New Revised Standard Version Bible.* 7th Edition. Bibleworks for Windows, 1989.

Chryssavgis, John. *In the Heart of the Desert: The Spirituality of the Desert Fathers and Mathers.* Bloomington: World Wisdom, Inc., 2003.

Chryssavgis, John, and Pachmios (Robert) Penkett, . *Abba Isaiah of Scetis Ascetic Discourses.* Kalamazoo: Cistercian Publications, 2002.

Colobos, St. John. *Saint Paisios the Great.* Translated by Leonidas Papadopulos and Georgia Lizardos. Jordanville:

Holy Trinity Monastery, 1983.

Corinth, St. Nikodimos of the Holy Mountain and St. Makarios of, ed. *The Philokalia: The Complete Text.* Translated by G.E.H Palmer, P Sherrard and K. Ware. Vol. 4 volumes. London: Faber and Faber Ltd., 1979-95.

El-Soriany, Fr Samaan. *The Hermit Fathers.* Marrickville: South Wood Press, 1993.

H G Bishop Serapion, and H G Bishop Youssef. *The Divine Liturgies: The Anaphoras of Saints Basil, Gregory, and Cyril.* 2nd Edition. Dallas: Coptic Orthodox Diocese of the Southern United States, 2007.

Hanna, Fr. Markos, trans. *The Coptic Offices for the Coptic Orthodox Church. Part 1: Bathing, Baptism, Holy Chrism.* Los Angeles: St. Mark Coptic Orthodox Church, 1995.

—. *The Holy Fathers in the Diptych of the Holy Divine Liturgy.* Los Angelos: St. Mark Coptic Orthodox Church, 1994.

Hansbury, Mary, trans. *The Letters of John of Dalyatha.* Piscataway: Gorgias Press LLC, 2006.

Hausherr, Irenee. *Spiritual Direction in the Early Christian East.* Translated by Anthony Gythiel. Kalamazoo: Cistercian Publications, 1990.

Library, Ages Digital. *Touch and Go Librarian: The Master Christian Library Version 6.* Albany, 1998.

Malaty, Fr. Tadros. *Anba Abraam the Friend of the Poor (1829 - 1914).* Santa Monica: St. Peter and St. Paul Coptic Orthodox, 1995.

Miller, Dana, trans. *The Ascetical Homilies of St. Isaac the Syrian.* Boston: Holy Transfiguration Monastery, 1984.

Nineveh, Isaac Bishop of. *The Second Part: Chapters IV–XLI.* Translated by Sebastian Brock. Lovanii: In Audibus Peeters, 1995.

Payne, R J, ed. *John Climacus: The Ladder of Divine Ascent.* Translated by C Luibheid and N Russell. Mahwah: Paulist Press, 1982.

Ramfos, Stelios. *Like a Pelican in the Wilderness: Reflections on the Sayings of the Desert Fathers.* Translated by Norman Russell. Brookline: Holy Cross Orthodox Press, 2000.

Russell, Norman, trans. *The Lives of the Desert Fathers: The Hostoria Monachorum in Aegypto.* Kalamazoo: Cistercian

Publications, 1981.

Shenouda III, HH Pope. *Calmness*. Cairo: COEPA, 1997.

—. *The Release of the Spirit*. Translated by Wedad Abbas. Sydney: COEPA, 1997.

Spidlik, Thomas. *Drinking from the Hidden Fountain*. Kalamazoo: Cistercian Publications, 1994.

St. Mark and St. Bishoy Coptic Orthodox Church. *Coptic Synaxarium*. IV vols. Illinois: St. Mark and St. Bishoy COC, 1987.

The Holy Psalmody. Ridgewood: Saint Mary and Saint Antonios Coptic Orthodox Church, 1990.

The New King James Version. Nashville: Thomas Nelson, Inc, 1982.

Thornton, J, and Varenne S, . *The Desert Fathers: Translations from the Latin*. Translated by Helen Waddell. New York: Vintage Books, 1998.

Vivian, Tim, trans. *Journeying into God: Seven Early Monastic Lives*. Minneapolis: Fortress Press, 1996.

Vivian, Tim, trans. *Saint Macarius the Spiritbearer: Coptic Texts Relating to Saint Macarius the Great*. Crestwood: St Vladimir's Seminary Press, 2004.

Vivian, Tim, ed. *Witness to holiness : Abba Daniel of Scetis : translations of the Greek, Coptic, Ethiopic, Syriac, Armenian, Latin, Old Church Slavonic, and Arabic accounts*. Translated by Sebastian Brock. Kalamazoo: Cistercian Publications, 2008.

Vlachos, Archim. Hierotheos. *A Night in the Desert of the Holy Mountain: Discussion with a Hermit on the Jesus Prayer*. Translated by Effie Mavromichali. Levadia: Birth of Theotokos Monastery, 1994.

Vlachos, B Hierotheos. *Othodox Psychotherapy*. Translated by Esther Williams. Levadia: Birth of the Theotokos Monastery, 1995.

Wansbrough, Henry, ed. *New Jerusalem Bible*. Random House, Inc, 1985.

Ward, Benedicta, trans. *The Desert Fathers: Sayings of the Early Christian Monks*. London: Penguin Books, 2003.

Ward, Benedicta, trans. *The Sayings of the Desert Fathers: The Alphabetical Collection*. Revised Edition. Kalamazoo: Cistercian Publications, 1984.

Ward, Benedicta, trans. *The Wisdom of the Desert Fathers: Systematic Sayings from the Anonymous Series of the Apophthegmata Patrum.* Fairacres: SLG Press, 1997.

Wheeler, Eric P, trans. *Dorotheos of Gaza.* Kalamazoo: Cistercian Publications, 1977.